The Legacy of Anne Conway (1631–1679)

The Legacy of Anne Conway (1631–1679)

Reverberations from a Mystical Naturalism

CAROL WAYNE WHITE

State University of New York Press

Published by
State University of New York Press, Albany

For information, contact State University of New York Press, Albany, NY
www.sunypress.edu

Production by Ryan Morris
Marketing by Anne M. Valentine

Library of Congress Cataloging-in-Publication Data

White, Carol Wayne, 1962–
    The legacy of Anne Conway (1631–1679) : reverberations from a
mystical naturalism / Carol Wayne White.
        p. cm.
    Includes bibiographical references and index.
    ISBN 978-0-7914-7465-5 (hardcover : alk. paper)
    ISBN 978-0-7914-7466-2 (pbk. : alk. paper)
    1. Conway, Anne, 1631–1679.   2. Philosophy of nature.   3. Nature—
Religious aspects—Christianity.   4. Naturalism.   5. Mysticism.   I. Title.

B1201.C5534W45 2008
192—dc22   2007035214

10 9 8 7 6 5 4 3 2 1

To the loving memory of Luther White, Jr.
and
to Jannie Mae White

Contents

Preface   ix
Acknowledgments   xiii

Part 1
Chapter 1   Anne Conway and Her Contemporaries   3

Chapter 2   Esoteric Knowledge, Practical Mysticism, and
             Embodied Love   11

Chapter 3   Conway, Descartes, and the New Mechanical
             Science   39

Part 2
Chapter 4   Conway's Religious Vitalism, Visionary
             Countertraditions, and the "More" of Life   63

Chapter 5   Processing Conway's Religious Naturalism   81

Chapter 6   Cultural Reverberations: Love, Religious
             Naturalism, and Feminism   97

Notes   119

Bibliography   141

Index   153

Preface

Anne Conway was an early modern religious philosopher whose life and ideas remain relatively unknown to the majority of contemporary Westerners. This is unfortunate because her published text *The Principles of the Most Ancient and Modern Philosophy* is, among other things, an intriguing seventeenth-century cosmological study outlining Conway's views on the nature of divinity, humanity, and the created order. Derived in part from her readings in the Lurianic Kabbalah, Conway's radical theological views challenged the Christian orthodoxy of her day and attempted to find a more naturalistic and pluralistic approach to many influential religious doctrines. Moreover, Conway's theory of monads, her attraction and eventual conversion to Quakerism, and her use of the Lurianic Kabbalah in developing her religious cosmology characterize her as an innovative and bold thinker—unusual qualities associated with women in the early modern period.

In this study, I recover Conway's ideas within the context of seventeenth-century English cultural and intellectual life and discuss her role in the history of the early Quakers. I also demonstrate the affinity between Conway's system of thought and contemporary concerns in religious naturalism. Conway's critique of the philosophy of her day (especially Descartes' mechanical theory) and her vitalistic theories regarding nature contained important ethical principles and conceptual innovations. Her early modern perspectives thus provide a remarkable antecedent for new naturalistic impulses in religious studies, particularly current reconstructions of nature that challenge "dominion-over-nature" ideologies derived from early scientific and modern conceptions. In short, Conway's vitalism has heuristic value, lending support in crucial ways to various reconstructions of nature in our current age. As a philosopher of religion, I have become increasingly convinced that the tenability of religious valuing today, depends, on part, on its capacity to move beyond deficient models of nature that have dominated mainstream thought until quite recently. As

Conway did in her era, I propose distinct approaches to the concept of nature that proclaim (in a host of ways) a subjectivity of nature. One minor aim of this study, therefore, is encouraging contemporary Westerners to view humans as natural processes in relation with other forms of sentient nature.

This study is divided into two major sections and has six chapters. Part 1 (composed of the first three chapters) is historical in presentation, focusing on Conway's key ideas within the context of seventeenth-century English intellectual and cultural life. Chapter 1 provides an introduction to Anne Conway, outlining the key elements of her life and sketching the general intellectual debates and developments that provide a backdrop for her ideas. I also discuss the prevalence of gender bias in seventeenth-century England to show the import of Conway's unique voice.

In chapter 2, I discuss Conway's interest in, and eventual conversion to, Quakerism, which I see as an important social corollary of her religious naturalism. I suggest that Conway's absorption of the Quakers' practical mysticism led to her eventual break with Henry More and his conservative theological tendencies, providing an opening for tracing the radical political force of her religious naturalism. In this chapter, I also examine Conway's interest in kabbalistic esotericism and its impact on her overall religious cosmology.

In chapter 3, I provide a critical reading of *The Principles of the Most Ancient and Modern Philosophy,* presenting Conway's relational view of nature and examining it within the context of Conway's Christian heritage and her basic philosophical convictions. I also examine Conway's critical response to Descartes' mechanistic philosophy, discussing select Cartesian principles that she both rejected and appropriated.

Part 2 addresses the heuristic value of Conway's religious vitalism for contemporary trends in religious naturalism. In chapter 4, I set vitalism within historical perspective, discussing influential conceptions of it that both preceded and followed Conway's own formulation. In addition, I present the themes and perspectives of select visionaries, poets, and scientists whose visions and conceptualizations of nature have been, like Conway's, unabashedly antireductionistic and capacious. In one manner or another, these figures have celebrated the fullness and abundant vitality of natural processes.

In chapter 5, I specifically identify reverberations of Conway's mystical view of nature within strains of twentieth-century process thought, suggesting, minimally, a potential connection between some early modern and postmodern models of religious naturalism.

Finally, in chapter 6, I outline key feminist themes that address dualist conceptualizations and exploitative treatments of myriad nature in its varied forms. Here, I focus on feminist religious scholarship that recovers the emphasis on relationality that is at the heart of Conway's cosmological views, and conclude by outlining a postmodern religious naturalism that addresses racial, gender, and ecological injustices.

Acknowledgments

It is a pleasure to express my gratitude to the persons and organizations that have lent support and contributed to the publication of this work. Chapters 2 and 5 have appeared in earlier forms as published chapters. I acknowledge the permission of Transaction Publishers to reprint from my essay "Valuing Nature: Vital Reconstructions of Anne Conway (1631–1679)" (Copyright © 2004 by Transaction Publishers; reprinted by permission of the publisher); and of SUNY Press to reprint materials from my chapter "Processing Henry Nelson Wieman: Creative Interchange Among Naturalism, Postmodernism, and Religion" (from *Process and Difference,* ed. Catherine Keller and Anne Daniell. Copyright © 2002 by SUNY Press).

I enjoyed working with Nancy Ellegate and the editorial staff at SUNY Press, and am thankful for the care with which they reviewed the original manuscript. I am also grateful to the anonymous reviewers whose insightful comments and suggestions helped improve the manuscript. I also acknowledge the encouragement and support of various colleagues who heard me present early papers on Anne Conway, especially my 2001 research colleagues at the Five College Women's Research Center at Mt. Holyoke College and Catherine Keller of Drew University. I am particularly grateful to my wonderful colleague and dear friend Maria Antonaccio for her steady encouragement and support of my work; and for the many stimulating conversations we have shared at Bucknell.

Finally, I offer a special word of thanks to Saundra Morris, who has been a brilliant presence in my life. I am grateful for her love, friendship, and support. And, I wish to express my profound thanks to Jannie Mae White for her enthusiastic support of my scholarly life and for being such a loving mother.

PART 1

CHAPTER 1

Anne Conway and Her Contemporaries

Though your ladyship has lived in the dark much, yett you have not at all liv'd in obscurity, your virtues and sufferings having made you as famous as any in the Nation.

—Henry More, *The Conway Letters*

During the seventeenth century in Western Europe, the nature and direction of developments in science (or natural philosophy) were matters of intense debate and investigation. This was also an era in which women could not attend university and their roles were restricted to that of wife and mother. It is surprising, therefore, to discover that Anne Conway, a seventeenth-century English philosopher, made important contributions to conversations about the nature and constitution of the physical world. The mechanical philosophies of Rene Descartes and Thomas Hobbes occupied center stage throughout the middle part of the seventeenth century, receiving much attention from philosophers and thinkers of diverse persuasions. In her sole published text, *The Principles of the Most Ancient and Modern Philosophy,* Conway challenged the basic assumptions of Descartes' dualism and advanced her own system as the true, most adequate philosophy of the time.[1] Conway anticipated many of the dangerous implications of the hierarchic dualisms associated with mind/matter and spirit/flesh distinctions. Assuming an anti-Hobbesian stance, she asserted that all

3

substances have some element, or at least potential possession, of thought or mentality. Conway's religious philosophy placed emphasis on the life of all things and compelled its adherents to adopt an ethic of care for the inherent worth of everything alive.

Unfortunately, Conway is better known for her lifelong head-aches that exhausted the resources of seventeenth-century medicine than for her contributions to natural philosophy.[2] In a gesture typical of patriarchal constructions of history, Conway's views on nature have been virtually erased from Western intellectual history and overshad-owed by a tradition of scientific views on nature inaugurated by such luminaries as Bacon, Hobbes, and Descartes. Moreover, *The Principles of the Most Ancient and Modern Philosophy* is not featured in most his-torical studies that trace the long-standing interconnections between religion and science.[3] The result is that Conway's distinct perspectives on the major categories concerning the "nature" of nature (substance, mind, matter, and time) have been ignored by most historians of phi-losophy and science, and her religious naturalism is practically un-known by contemporary religious scholars.

In this study, I recover Conway's ideas concerning nature, con-tending that they are too important to remain in obscurity.[4] I do so for several reasons. First, Conway's views increase our awareness of the diversity of intellectual positions regarding the construction of nature during the seventeenth century. Her published treatise shows that at least one woman provided a provocative articulation of natural phi-losophy and offered a sustained critique of mechanistic science. This fact helps to dismiss the still popular (and unfounded) notion that women were not significant contributors to essential debates concern-ing natural processes during the early modern period. Second, Conway constructs an alternative cosmology to the mechanistic worldview popularized by Descartes and others. In so doing, she offers a reli-gious cosmology resonating with ethical force regarding proper rela-tions among all forms of nature. Third, I believe Conway's cosmological views foreshadow a trajectory of religious naturalism that has chal-lenged the "dominion-over-nature" ideology derived from the mod-ern scientific conception of nature that began with Bacon and escalated horrifically throughout the eighteenth and nineteenth centuries. Conway's reflections on the "sentience" of nature prefigure some key assumptions and implications of twentieth-century process cosmologies regarding the radical relationality found among all forms of nature.

Finally, Conway's general outlook is consistent with my own basic convictions as a philosopher of religion, namely, that religious truths are conditioned by beliefs about (human) nature and destiny—

that is, by what we think about ourselves as natural processes in relation to other natural processes surrounding us. Conway's historical example thus lends support in crucial ways to current projects that reenvision the relationality of nature in our own "post" age. Conway's work thus provides a surprising antecedent for new naturalistic impulses in religious studies as some of us call into question the deficient scientific models of nature that have dominated mainstream thought until quite recently.

THE FAMOUS CASE OF LADY ANNE CONWAY

Anne Conway was born Anne Finch on December 14, 1631, into a politically influential and prominent English family.[5] She was the younger of two children of Elizabeth Craddock and Sir Heneage Finch, Sergeant-at-Law, Recorder of the City of London, and Speaker of the House of Commons. Both parents had been married before and widowed: her mother to Richard Benet, her father to Frances Bell, by whom he had seven sons and four daughters. According to the various biographical sketches of her life, Conway was not bound by conventional "feminine" duties, and hence spent most of her time studying Latin and Greek, and reading voraciously in philosophical and classical literature.

Conway's passion for learning was so intense that the mysterious headaches that plagued her from age twelve were initially attributed to her excessive studying habits.[6] Her brother, John Finch, also encouraged Conway's learning through gifts of books and involvement in philosophical discussions. Conway married at age nineteen, and her husband, Viscount Edward Conway (1623–83) who was away often on business trips, also supported his wife's intellectual endeavors. When their only child, a son, died in infancy, Conway had even more time for reading and study. As well, her father-in-law, Lord Conway, known as a collector of books and a gentleman of diverse intellectual interests, enjoyed lively conversations with Conway. Their correspondence reveals animated debates on diverse perspectives and topics ranging from Copernican astronomy and Pythagorean maxims, through Henry Wotton's architectural theory, to the literary writings of John Donne and scriptural and apocryphal texts.[7] Through the influence of her brother John, who had been a student at Christ's College, Cambridge, Conway became the (long-distance) pupil of the leading Cambridge Platonist, Henry More (1614–87), with whom she maintained a close and respectful intellectual friendship for over thirty-five years.

More often praised Conway's intellectual gifts and her brilliance, even dedicating one of his important writings, *Antidote to Atheism* (1652), to her.

As Conway gained respect for her erudition, her bouts with pain were so severe and mysterious that she also became a famous medical case. Through the years, her family sought relief for Conway from among the leading medical minds of the day—the family's personal physician was William Harvey, discoverer of the circulation of blood—but to no avail. Thomas Willis of Oxford eventually diagnosed and predicted chronic, unceasing pain for Conway for the duration of her life. In 1665, as England was struck by the plague, Conway's headaches became so severe and debilitating that she and her husband sought the help of Valentine Greatrakes, a healer in Ireland rumored to cure people simply by laying his hands on them. After much discussion and pleading from the Conways, Greatrakes journeyed to England to visit and cure Conway, arriving at Ragley Hall (Conway's estate in Warwickshire) on January 27, 1665. Among those gathered to witness the great event were Henry More, Ralph Cudworth, and Benjamin Whichcote, all of whom were keenly interested in such unexplainable healings. Before attempting to treat Lady Conway, Greatrakes healed some of the tenants present, making his prospects for aiding Conway even more likely and remarkable. When, however, Greatrakes tried to heal Conway, he failed.

Five years later, another prominent figure, and perhaps one of the most colorful characters of the seventeenth century, entered Conway's life: Francis Mercury van Helmont (1614–98), the gypsy scholar.[8] Van Helmont was the son of the famous chemist Jean Baptiste van Helmont, and first encountered Conway through the intervention of More. In October 1670, while entertaining van Helmont at Christ's Church in Cambridge, More described Conway's debilitating headaches to the wandering physician. Impressed with van Helmont's reputation as an alchemist and miraculous healer, More then invited the physician to visit Conway in Warwickshire to see if he could offer any relief from the persistent headaches affecting his beloved student.[9] Upon his arrival at Ragley that winter, however, van Helmont was unsuccessful in treating or curing Conway's headaches, as was the experience of Greatrakes five years earlier.

Van Helmont soon became Conway's closest friend as well as her personal physician, living continuously at Ragley beginning in 1671. A unique intellectual bond between the two began during this time as Conway and van Helmont explored intriguing doctrines developed from alchemy, the Kabbalah, and other esoteric literature and philosophies. Their creative exchanges eventually compelled Conway to move away from the dualism of her early Cartesian studies and to revise the traditional philosophic knowledge provided by More. Conway and van Helmont also eventually became Quakers, a monumental decision that was deplored by both More and members of Conway's family.

Van Helmont's devotion to Conway and the extraordinary intimacy between the two are clearly evident in the fascinating events surrounding her death in 1679. While Conway's husband was away in Ireland attending to his large estates, van Helmont preserved Conway's corpse in spirits of wine in the library at Ragley until her husband's return. Although scholars acknowledge that it is difficult to access precisely how, and to what extent, van Helmont was also instrumental in transforming Conway's philosophical notes into *The Principles* several years after her death. Whether prepared by van Helmont or More individually or jointly (or by a third party, under their supervision), van Helmont had a Latin text of Conway's work ready for publication by 1690.

INTELLECTUAL WOMEN AND WRITING IN SEVENTEENTH-CENTURY ENGLAND

Conway's intellectual development and the philosophical and religious innovations at Ragley appear anomalous in the context of seventeenth-century English society. The ideals of Renaissance humanism, which extended to women the right to learn, had been lost, and the Tudor emphasis on erudition was now in disfavor. In nearly every country of seventeenth-century Europe, an educated woman was frowned upon and viewed as a social misfit, and a "woman" philosopher fully ostracized. A pejorative term—bluestocking—was even coined to designate the female intellectual, or the woman who pursued the "manly" goals of studying philosophy. The only females mentioned in Abraham Cowley's prospectus for a new college where philosophy would specifically be studied were "four old women to tend the chambers and such like services."[10] His projected budget allocated ten pounds for such women's work, the least amount for all servants—with the ten pounds evenly divided among them. Cowley's example is paradigmatic of the structural and systematic forces at work in the seventeenth century that kept women financially dependent on men, making them feel intellectually inferior to their male counterparts.

Women who dared to publish their theoretical writings were often mocked, attacked, or jeered by critics, as in the case with Lady Margaret Cavendish of Newcastle, a contemporary of Conway's. Cavendish was ridiculed, and often referred to as Mad Madge, for publishing works dealing with science and philosophy.[11] Along with other women, Cavendish protested against the gender biases surrounding women's education, and the lack of access to formal knowledge:

> . . . .for the most part women are not educated as they should be, I mean those of quality, for their education is only to dance, sing, and fiddle, to write complimental letters, to read romances, to speak some language that is not their native, which education, is an education of the body, and not of the mind, and shows that their parents take more care of their feet than their head, more of their words than their reason, more of their music than their virtue, more of their beauty than their honesty, which methinks is strange, as that their friends and parents would take more care, and be at greater charge to adorn their bodies, than to endue their minds.[12]

Bathsua Makin, a seventeenth-century reformer, also deplored the sad neglect of women's formal education in her own century. Reminiscing on the halcyon days of Tudor England, when a woman's erudition was a favorable asset, Makin objected to the double standard in educational practices in *An Essay to Revive the Anteint Education of Gentlewomen in Religion, Manners, Arts and Tongues*:

> Custom, when it is inveterate, has a mighty influence: it has the force of Nature itself. The barbarous custom to breed women low, is grown general amongst us, and hath prevailed so far, that it is verily believed (especially amongst a sort of debauched sots) that women are not endued with such reason as men; nor capable of improvement by education, as they are. . . . A learned woman is thought to be a comet, that bodes mischief whenever it appears.[13]

Makin reiterated a theme that would become a dominant one among those women who published literary or other sorts of polemical texts during this period. Emphasizing the inadequate academic instruction granted to seventeenth-century women, and forecasting the cultural and social benefits for both sexes if this gender disparity were to change, she wrote, "I verily think, women were formerly educated in the knowledge of arts and tongues, and by their education, many did rise to a great height in learning. Were women thus educated now, I am confident the advantage would be very great, the women would have honor and pleasure, their relations profit, and the whole nation advantage."[14]

Although misogynist biases and practices prevented all women from entering the traditionally masculine domain of the university (the thought of a woman entering Cambridge or Oxford was inconceivable), Conway and some other women overcame such restrictions and contributed greatly to the intellectual developments of the period. With diverse styles and approaches, and with varying degrees of radicalism and public acceptance, these scholarly women conceived and published works on key issues that often challenged, and sometimes supplemented, the academic knowledge advanced by the elite male establishment.[15]

Conway did not have a prototypical public voice, as found in such women as Cavendish and Makin, yet she was greatly influential in her own quiet way. Here, it is important to acknowledge the extent to which van Helmont, More, and countless others, took note of Conway's words and ideas during the intellectual salons held at Ragley. For example, van Helmont's genuine admiration of Conway's philosophical depth and her unique religious cosmology was often reflected in his sharing of her insights and ideas with others.[16] Having been introduced to her work by van Helmont, Gottfried Willhelm Leibniz wrote: *Les miens en philosophie approchent un peu d'advantage de ceux de feu Madame la Comtesse de Conway, et tiennent le milieu entre Platon et Democrite, puisque je crois que tout se fait mechaniquement, comme veulent Democrite et Descartes, contre l'opinion de Mr. Morus et ses semblabes; et que neanmoins tout se fait encore vitalement et suivant les causes finales, tout etant plein de vie et perception, contre l'opinion des Democritiens."*[17] Beyond such acknowledgments, the provocative, brilliant charisma of Conway as a "woman" philosopher and religious innovator was especially evident in her complex system of thought, which provides crucial and diverse forms of knowledge regarding nature in the seventeenth century.

CHAPTER 2

Esoteric Knowledge, Practical Mysticism, and Embodied Love

On the plain leaden cover someone has scratched two words: "Quaker Lady." It is her only epitaph.

—Marjorie Hope Nicolson, *The Conway Letters*

Conway's illness and love of philosophical discussion put her into contact (either directly or indirectly) with persons representing a wide range of intellectual, social, and religious positions: spiritualists, physicians, kabbalists, Cambridge Platonists, and Quakers. As a result of these encounters, Conway's home (Ragley Hall) became the epicenter of intellectual and theological innovations, as well as a haven of social progressiveness. Her "salon" was a darkened bedroom where, too weak to raise her head, Conway held captive the leading intellectuals and thinkers of her day, including van Helmont and More. The usual private/public dichotomy of early modern life, which relegated women's essential activity to the former and men's to the latter, took on an interesting twist as Conway entertained a variety of ideas and individuals in her home, indeed often in her bedroom. What is so remarkable about this situation is that a traditional marker of domesticity (the home) is transformed into an intellectual and discursive site. The unusual developments, conversations, and collaborative projects

11

occurring at Conway's homestead are a crucial part of seventeenth-century cultural and religious history that has been overlooked. This is unfortunate because at Ragley, traditional gender and class hierarchies were destabilized, and theological orthodoxies dismantled, as Conway and her friends pursued radical, provocative notions of love and yearned for true experiences of divinity.

Conway's individual quest began with her investigation of esoteric wisdoms and culminated in the religious choice of her later years: Quakerism. With van Helmont, she also experimented with an innovative conception of love, characterized in *The Principles* as a basic movement of nature toward the divine. Yet, for Conway, love (whether divine or otherwise) was not a mere abstraction; rather, it took on specific ethical force and experiential depth, shaped, in part, by her experiences with the early Quaker movement and by her study of the Kabbalah. What I am suggesting is that Conway's quest for divinity remains at the center of crucial religious developments that warrant further exploration.

The most complete record we have of Conway's encounters with the Quakers, and of her intellectual activity aside from her text, is the collection of letters compiled by Marjorie Hope Nicolson: *The Conway Letters: The Correspondence of Anne, Viscountess Conway, Henry More, and their Friends (1642–1684)*.[1] These letters help bring out nuances of meaning and conceptual innovations assumed in *The Principles*. They also provide a fuller account of the social and political dimensions of Conway's thought, demonstrating an important social corollary of her religious naturalism. In this chapter, I draw heavily upon those written during the last years of Conway's life (1670–79) in discussing her encounters with Quaker religiosity and outlining her explorations of the Lurianic Kabbalah.

CONWAY AND MORE ADDRESS
ENTHUSIASTIC RELIGION AND RADICAL LOVE

Years after More ceased to be Conway's tutor, he remained dedicated to her, often visiting her at her estate in Warwickshire whenever his busy writing schedule allowed and engaging other visitors who happened to be present. When apart, More and Conway corresponded with each other, recounting and discussing specific events in their respective lives in Cambridge and at Ragley in Warwickshire. While Conway's earliest correspondence with More revealed an impressionable young student, those written between 1670 and 1677 depicted intimate, fond exchanges between an older, more independent woman and an elderly friend who was genuinely enamored of his former student's intellectual capacities.[2] During these years, the two discussed matters ranging from mundane daily concerns of health, through general philosophical disputes and ideas, to provocative theological discussions. In specific letters, for example, they made reference to such diverse issues as Descartes' *Principia,* Islamic theology, and kabbalistic teachings.[3] In others, More received encouragement and spiritual advice from Conway, who often reflected on her physical sufferings. More was very attentive to Conway's illness, frequently expressing consolation and well wishes: "I am very sorry your Ladiship has so little intermission from your inveterate distemper. And I would not that you should adde any further affliction to yourself by over much anxiety touching the welfare of your friends abroad."[4] On more than one occasion, after commenting on the frailties of the body, More evoked the presence of God and encouraged Conway to trust solely in divine power for respite and rejuvenation.

Accounts of Conway's chronic sufferings were not confined to her correspondence with More, however; other individuals also inquired of her health and often asked whether the medical treatment from van Helmont was working. In one response to her brother-in-law, Sir George Rawdon, Conway showed her growing indebtedness to the physician's presence in her life:

> To your kinde enquiry after what ease I find from Monsieur van Hellmont, I must give this account, my paines and weakness does certainly increase daily, but yett I doubt not, but I have had some releef (God bee thanked) from his medicines, I am sure more than I ever had from ye endeavours of any person whatsoever else, but yett I have had much more satisfaction in his company, he has yet ye patience to continue wth mee in my solitude, wch makes it ye easier to mee, none of my own relations having ye leasure to afford mee yt comfort, and indeed I think very few friends could have ye patience to doe it in ye circumstances that I am in, wch makes my obligations to him so much ye greater.[5]

Conway's relationship with More became increasingly strained during the last four years of her life due to her increasing interest in esoteric theological and philosophical ideas, which she shared with van Helmont. Before van Helmont arrived at Ragley in 1670 to treat her, Conway had been reading the provocative mystical writings associated with Jacobe Behoeme and Henry Nicholas, the founder of the

"Family of Love." Van Hemont thus provided the perfect intellectual comrade for Conway, for he, too, was intrigued by mystical literature, including the Kabbalah, having explored these forms of knowledge during his many travels and in his profession as a physician. For the next nine years (1671–79), van Helmont and Conway studied esoteric and occult matters, experimented with ideas that departed from Orthodox Christianity of the period, and shared a love of nonconventional metaphysics. Their rare, intimate friendship and shared interests led to a noticeable change in More's relationship with Conway. Reading Conway's reports of her growing receptivity to the ideas of such groups as the Familists and Quakers made More increasingly upset and anxious. Wary of any "truth" emerging from the teachings of the Familists and Quakers, the good doctor viewed their doctrines inappropriate for a woman of Conway's erudition and social standing.

More's opinion of these groups was not uncommon for someone of his social class and educational training. The Familists and Quakers were included among the various sects and dissenters (Seekers, English Baptists, Levelers, Diggers, Muggletonians, Socinians, and Ranters) that rose during the Interregnum, representing a variety of religious, political, social, and economic reforms.[6] Some of these groups disagreed with the beliefs and practices of the Church of England, focusing their energies on creating new doctrines and forms of worship. Other dissenters rallied against myriad forms of political and economic oppressions. A major target for some dissenters was the organized clergy's use of scholarship, which they felt was merely a tool to make simple religion inaccessible to the masses, both concealing and enhancing the clergy's own role as exploiters who maintained the power of the ruling class. Consequently, most leaders and citizens of the upper social echelons generally experienced these groups as dangerous anarchistic rebels—at worst, a destabilizing presence to local and national governments.

As a typical learned Englishman with social privilege, More symbolized his peers' general suspicion of the Familists and the Quakers, whom he felt epitomized the grave error of the enthusiasts of the Civil War years. The Familists and Quakers thus became major topics in much of the later correspondence between Conway and More as they debated whether or not the Quakers emerged from, or were similar to, the Familists in religious fervor and doctrine. In many of More's letters to Conway written between 1669 and 1671 are found the initials "H. N.," signifying Henry Nicholas, to whom More also traced the origins of early Quaker religion.[7] There is scant information on Nicholas' life, but the available information suggests that he was born in either 1501 or 1502 in Westphalia. In 1530, after imprisonment for heresy, Nicholas departed for Amsterdam; a few years later, in 1540, Nicholas announced that he had received a divine message encouraging him to found the *Familia Caritatis*.[8]

According to historian Rufus Jones, the Familists, interchangeably known as the Family of Love, or House of Love, were unique among the various sects flourishing during the early seventeenth century, and also vilified by many of their peers for their specific doctrines and practices. Creating a very lofty type of mystical religiosity, Nicholas advocated a doctrine of love, describing it sometimes as the "light of the world," or as the "bread of life." Those dwelling in love, he taught, lived according to the divine commandments. Nicholas' concept of love was directly associated with his provocative view that people could completely conquer sin and become divine.[9] According to his theological system, women and men could regain in this life the innocence and freedom from sin that belonged to prefallen humanity, as recalled in the Edenic myth. For many of his peers, Nicholas' idea of humans perfecting themselves was heretical foolishness and approached pantheism. For example, John Knewstub, the Puritan leader, reproached Nicholas' views, stating, "H.N. turns religion upside down. He buildeth heaven here upon earth; he maketh God man and man God."[10]

Cultivating a radical anticlericalism, Nicholas also taught that only the spirit of God within the Christian could understand scripture, thus emphasizing the importance of an itinerant apostolic priesthood. The social radicalism of his religious system was also evident in his notion that property should be held in common—a view that would become a central feature of later nineteenth-century experiments in social utopians that flowered in the United States. English translations of Nicholas' writings were readily available in London by the mid-fifties and sixties; however, the Council of Trent prohibited them in 1570 and 1582, and later, in 1590, by a papal bull. In 1580, Queen Elizabeth issued a proclamation condemning the Familists and their writings. Due to these prohibitions, the Familists were repeatedly attacked in the seventeenth century and became a convenient group on which to heap all the fury and disgust the orthodox had for deviant sects.

More was also very familiar with Nicholas' writings; however, unlike Conway, he despised Nicholas' enthusiasm. In a letter he wrote in 1669 to Elizabeth Foxcraft, who often kept Conway company at Ragley, More first condemned Nicholas' teachings as heretical, and then lambasted the Quakers for their ludicrous hypocrisy and boastfulness.

> As goodly as he lookes he is an Infidell or Pagan canting in Scripture phrases, and in the outward dresse and termes of our Christian Religion, really undermining the ancient Apostolick truth thereof, and under the pretense of crying up the upright life taking away the necessary prop thereof which is the ancient Apostolick Fayth, without which what pressing and effectuall incitements he can use to make men good I confesse I know not. . . . It is a hott, crude, bold confident high aspiring spirit in them, not the spirit of God, that setts them in the midst of their Infidelity above those that are more truly the members of Christ then themselves.[11]

One of More's primary reasons for linking the Quakers and the Familists was their failure to emphasize the historical basis of Christianity. Although he claimed to like individual Quakers, even admitting that he wished more Christians would imitate them, More was genuinely offended by their teachings and religious fervor, which he believed endangered the sacred order of things.[12] For More, such a threat to the social order was as dangerous as atheism itself. In a letter addressed to Conway in September 1670, he made an interesting analogy between the scholarly productivity of Thomas Hobbes and Nicholas; for More, both were immensely popular writers advancing dangerous ideas:

> And I thinke Hobbs has wrote as many books to promote Atheisme, as H. N. has to promote infidelity. And as the Admiration of men speeds Hobbes on his way, so the veneration of H. N.'s proselytes, for to him, besides the many gifts and his own conceit of himself, that he was the highest illuminated man in the world that ever was or could be (as Hobbes takes himself to be the Iob of philosophers), this made him with ease undergoe the pains of writing so many bookes, as those gifts enabled him to weare a Satin dubblet, though he was but an ordinarie Tradesman.[13]

More's crusade against religious enthusiasm began in the 1650s when he had first attacked the alchemical writings of Thomas Vaughan. In several early writings, he also addressed the symptoms, causes, and cure of enthusiasm, intent on defending its true manifestation, namely, Christian deification, from the phenomenon he believed was produced by natural causes and symbolized by moral and physical disease.[14] In *Enthusiasmus Triumphatus* (1656), for example, More condemned religious radicals, especially political enthusiasts, who saw themselves as messengers of God.

Conway was not as quick as More to denounce all religious enthusiasm and often questioned his biased assumptions of Quaker religiosity. As late as 1675, the two were still debating the topic of religious enthusiasm, and the purported Quaker and Familist connection. In a letter written in early January, More asserted,

> Methinkes that your Ladiship is over sure in that point, that the Quakers from the beginning had nothing to do with Familisme. The carriage of James Naylour, who was then at least equall with Fox, is to me a demonstration of how much at least many of them were tinctured with Familisme. And I was told by one, when I went up to London last, who was acquainted with the Familists, and in a maner received into their sect, that these very Familists that he was acquainted withall, to the number of about twenty, was downright Quakers as soone as that forme appeared. And I must confesse I always looked upon them as Familists onely armed with rudenesse and an obstinate Activity.[15]

More's description of the Quakers as heretical seemed unfair to Conway, who, along with van Helmont, had become genuinely intrigued by the purity of love exemplified by those Quakers she engaged at Ragley. Despite their eccentricities, they seemed to her to express a quiet yet pure expression of the divine that symbolized authentic Christianity.[16]

Conway's openness to the Quakers and rejection of her former mentor's views are noteworthy for several reasons. First, she assessed the authenticity of Quaker religiosity based on her own observations of and engagements with them rather than on the public and negative images upheld by More. With such independent thinking, Conway thus anticipated, or made a gesture toward, an important theological interpretive strategy, what later religious feminists would identify as a hermeneutic of suspicion. Such theological acuity helped Conway demystify and expose More's authorial ideological "reading" of the Quakers. Moreover, Conway's willingness to challenge traditional, established theological views—even More's—based on the fuller forms of truth and knowledge she intuited and experienced with the Quakers, reveals the potentially radical and political aspects of her mystical queries and embodied approach to truth.

Early Quakers in England (or Friends, as they were popularly known at that time) have been described in myriad ways: as founders of a fundamentally new form of spirituality, as rediscoverers of original Christianity, as radical inheritors of English Puritanism, and as political revolutionaries. Whatever the label, they expressed a distinctive religiosity that countered respectable social norms and sensibilities of English society. For example, Quakers refused to remove their hats to members of the higher class and rejected the customary titles of honor. They did not pay tithes on the principle that one should not financially support what one could not ethically endorse. Quakers also avoided taking legal oaths, rejecting the assumption that unless under oath, one was not obliged to tell the truth. (They did not distinguish between official and personal truth.) Members of the group even refused to serve in the military, often making no effort to defend themselves when they were confronted, repeatedly, with personal violence. Furthermore, these early Quakers were genuinely troubled by a societal ethos that cultivated desire for, and acquisition of, unnecessary ostentation for some while others were without basic necessities. With their simple language and form of worship, Quakers exposed the hierarchical and unjust standards of the period maintained by the religious orthodoxy. Their plain clothing was symbolic of a fundamental belief that inward integrity was much more important than outward pretension.[17] More had these countercultural images in mind as he wrote to Conway about the enthusiasm and irrationality of the Quakers. With her usual independence of thought and general kindness, Conway continually questioned More's vivid and harsh accusations against both Familists and Quakers, and urged him to read more and not be so hasty in drawing such negative conclusions.

Conway's perceptive challenges to More's anti-Quaker biases coincided with another interesting development at Ragley: van Helmont began attending Quaker meetings and engaging the group in a more intimate manner. In a postscript to a November 1675 letter to More, Conway inadvertently mentioned that van Helmont had become very fascinated by Quaker life; he was becoming "a very religious Churchman, he goes every Sunday to the Quaker meetings."[18] A visit with Lord Conway in London a month later to discuss a business matter provided More the opportunity to address van Helmont's situation and the increasing Quaker presence at Ragley. During the visit, Conway's husband shared with More some troubling news that had reached him from Warwickshire, namely, that his wife had become a Quaker. While consoling Lord Conway, More replied that his beloved, longtime friend was too sensible to join any sect. He shared this conversation with Conway in a letter, saying,

> I told my Lord, how little feare there is of your Ladiships turning Quaker, they haveing nothing better to communicate to you then you have already, and that you are not at all in love with their

rudenesse and clownishnesse. . . . I shall farther tomorrow morning conferr with my Lord about this buisinesse and ease his mind therein as well as I can. For I perceive he is much concerned in it, and it would be grievous to him, to phancy any such thing. But I am fully persuaded, your Ladiship has tasted of a better dispensation then to soile yourself by professing any sect, though you may lawfully and justly commend what good there is in any, that is holy righteous within, and no blott to your honour.[19]

More was aware that such rumors were due, in part, to the fact that van Helmont attended Quaker meetings and that Quakers frequently visited Ragley, so he wrote to Conway several weeks later, advising her not to follow van Helmont down a slippery slope of irrationality and passion. In this letter, dated December 29, More emphasized that one could appreciate some of the positive features of the Quakers without converting to their lifestyle, adding a word of advice for van Helmont: "And though Monsieur Van Helmont go to their meetings, yett I would advize him by all meanes to absteine from useing their garb in Hall or speech. Severall goe to heare them that never come to that, and have a kindnesse for them, although they partake not of their odnisses."[20]

Although More never accepted the Quakers as a whole, he did engage individual ones, befriending, for example, Robert Barclay and enjoying some type of correspondence with William Penn. More also engaged in theological debates with a few, conversing with John and George Whitehead as well as George Keith about specific Quaker notions.[21] With the exception of certain figures like Keith and the Whiteheads, most early Quakers did not ponder philosophical quandaries. Moreover, it was difficult to say with certainty what systematic theory the Quakers held—ascertaining any sustained theological truth among them was primarily gained through conversations with individual Quakers. In an earlier letter to Conway written in 1674, More had described a particular visit with Keith, whom he considered to be insightful and very bright:

> But I perswaded G. Keith when he came, both to supp with me and dine with me next day, and had I believe 9 or 12 hours discourse with him, and setting aside his Schismaticallnesse, which I roundly told him off, and the ridiculous rusticity of that sect, I found a man very considerably learned, of a good witt and quick apprehension, and which is best of all, heartily breathing after the attainment of the new life of a Christian. He is very philosophically and platonically given, and is pleased with the Notion of the Spiritt of Nature.[22]

Yet, in one as conceptually astute as Keith, More still detected a dis-
tasteful enthusiasm for teachings that he considered to be erroneous.
More's major critique of Keith was his doctrine of "Christ within,"
which More believed was pantheistic and dangerously heretical in its
forfeiture of the historical Christ. In his *An Explanation of the Grand
Mystery of Godliness* (1660), More had publicly objected to the doctrine
of "Christ within" because he thought it implied the awful notion that
Quakers deserved divine adoration.[23] Sometimes cryptic and harsh
when describing Keith's teachings, More nonetheless believed it was
his duty to lead Keith and other Quakers away from their error. Hence,
whether rejecting specific doctrines or defending his own interpretation of scriptural prophecy, More continually reiterated to Conway his
suspicion that the Quakers were linked to the Familists. On a more
positive note, despite the apparent doctrinal disagreements found in
sustained conversation with Keith and others, More acknowledged a
sincere search for truth among Keith and some Quakers.

More's confidence that he could converse with the Quakers without succumbing to their erroneous doctrines was not fully extended to
others, as his letters during the winter of 1675–76 evince. They show his
suspicions of the possible growing intimacy developing among van
Helmont, Conway, and the Quakers. In one letter written in January,
More continued to warn Conway of the dangers of sectarianism, specifically refuting George Keith's doctrine of Christ's soul extending through
the universe, as well as to suggest the most suitable dining arrange-
ments for Quakers visiting Ragley. In the postscript, More added, with
some anxiety: "Since my writing of this, I heare there are Quaker meetings at Ragley with Monsieur Van Helmont, but I sayd I thought it was
a mistake, and that it was occasion'd from Monsieur Van Helmont's
going to the Quakers meetings."[24] A month later, More received Conway's
detailed reply, which both denied the rumors and provided a very clear
statement of her interest in the Quakers. She wrote,

> I am not in love with the name of a Quaker nor yett wth what you
> terme their rusticity, but their principles and practices (at least
> most of them) as far as I am capable to judge are Christian and
> Apostolical; and the most of them as farr as I can see or hear live
> as they preach, which makes me hope (if my presage doe not
> deceive me) to be better served by such in my chamber, then I
> have yett been by any of any other profession, but of this I shall
> best judge after tryal, which I am now experiencing.[25]

Similar to More's experience with Conway, Lord Conway was
powerless in dissuading his wife from studying Quaker ideas or from

interacting with them. Hearing about the conversations at his home and in his absence, Lord Conway shared More's increasing concern that van Helmont really was a bad influence on his wife, seducing her with dangerous ideas and making her vulnerable to undesirable social stigma. Lord Conway's frustration and anger at the Quaker presence at Ragley, which he felt had been initiated by van Helmont and consequently allowed by his wife, were evident in a June 1676 letter he wrote to his brother-in-law during one visit home:

> Dr More, Mr Wilson and others dined with me today in the parlor at a very plentiful table, but Monsr. Van Helmont with six or seven Quakers dined in some other room in the house as plentifully as we, both for meat and wine, and nothing [wanted] of what we had, so they supped last night, and lodge here, and I never see them, and all their horses in the stables better fed than mine, and when I am absent the house is as full of them as it can hold. How long this will last I know not, for I have not yet seen my wife since I came, but both my own knowledge and from Dr More I can assure you that my wife is no Quaker. I know she is very much against persecuting them, and thinks some of them extraordinary good persons, and Monsr. Van Helmont hath wrought himself extremely into my wife's good opinion, so as to think him the necessariest person in the world about her. . . . To injure Monsr. Van Helmont is to injure my wife in the sensiblest part, but it is from him that the reproach of her being a Quaker and thousand other stories proceeds, and she says she is willing to bear it.[26]

Despite her husband's consternation, Conway continued to receive many Quakers into her home, reading their works and developing friendships with several prominent ones. George Fox, George Keith, Issac Pennington, Charles Lloyd, and many unnamed Quaker women were frequent visitors at Ragley between 1675 and 1677. Conway even corresponded with William Penn, who unceasingly advocated the essence of Quaker piety. In one letter to Conway, he wrote: "My Friend, Not only the generall fame of thy desires after the very best things, but thy perticuler kind invitations, have begotten in me very strong inclinations to see thee. . . . My friend, we preach not our selves, but the light of Christ in the conscience, which is gods faithfull and true wittness, that the worldly, pompous church has slain, and made merry over; and all thos that are in a fleshy religion (insensible of this pure light and spirit of Jesus) they are in Babilon, and, which is wors, of Babilon."[27]

RAGLEY HALL AS A CENTER OF INTELLECTUAL, SOCIAL, AND THEOLOGICAL INNOVATIONS

Among the Quakers who came to Ragley, George Keith had the most direct influence on Conway and van Helmont, and they on him. Keith had first come to Ragley in 1675 in place of William Penn, who was securing the release of Quakers prisoners before Parliament. Conway described this visit to More in a letter dated November 1675, showing her own personal interest in and growing devotion to the Quakers.

> George Keith gave me a visit in his journy to Scotland, I could not prevail with him to stay above 2 or 3 weekes, but that time I had while he was in the house, I spent with much satisfaction in his company (though I was very ill, and in my bed, when I did see him). I am glad, you had an opportunity of so free and full a converse with severall of these Quakers, when you were in London, by which meanes you will be able to give a better judgment of their principles and practices, then you could doe upon the reports of others, who either through prejudice or ignorance had doubtlessly misrepresented them to you. The reading of their bookes lately had in a great measure freed me from former prejudicate opinions, but their conversation doth much more reconcile me to them.[28]

In her interactions with Keith, Conway became even more appreciative of the unique and fascinating worldview the Quakers offered their contemporaries, namely, their emphasis on the light within, their belief in unmediated human communion with the divine, and their resistance to dry conventionality. She engaged Keith eagerly, delighting in his theological innovations and increasing her receptivity to the Quaker way of life.

In Keith, Conway and van Helmont found a kindred spirit, one also troubled by some of the same Christian teachings they were questioning. Keith also considered a theological problem that preoccupied Conway as well: How could Christianity be a universal religion if Christian soteriology required a belief in the historical figure of Jesus Christ? In *Immediate Revelation* (1663), Keith had argued that historical knowledge of Christ was not an essential aspect of Christian belief or behavior since "some people have been true Christians without having heard of Christ, while other who have heard of Christ have not been Christians at all."[29] He also emphasized the doctrine of "Christ within" as more indicative of true Christian piety than exact knowledge of scripture. Keith's reflections on Quaker ideas (e.g., notions of reason and revelation and the light within) were continually shaped by his long conversations at Ragley with both Conway and van Helmont. The extended exchanges among the three became the occasion for yet another innovative development in Ragley: the creative integration of Quaker mysticism with Lurianic Kabbalism.

The Lurianic Kabbalah was the definitive kabbalistic tradition in Western Europe during the seventeenth century, and much of what we know about it at that time is due to the efforts of Christian Knorr von Rosenroth (1636–89), a German Lutheran who had studied ancient rabbinical and Hebrew lore under the tutelage of a rabbi in Amsterdam.[30] Aided by van Helmont, von Rosenroth (whom More and Conway referred to as Peganius in their letters), translated and published the *Kabbala denudata*, a collection and translation of the largest number of kabbalistic texts available to the Latin-reading public until the nineteenth century; it was published in three parts: the first in 1677, the second in 1678, and the third in 1684. One of von Rosenroth's interest in publishing the *Kabbala denudata* was to offer a Latin translation of the key ideas found in the most famous kabbalistic work, the Zohar, while providing other kabbalistic treatises and commentaries to help readers understand the notoriously difficult text. As indicated by recent scholars, von Rosenroth's studies in Jewish mysticism were part of a larger, controversial Christian development in the seventeenth century with unabashed conversionist aims.[31] Von Rosenroth's Christian conversionist goals were quite clear throughout the *Kabbala denudata*, as well as in his other writings and correspondence, for he believed the Zohar provided answers to all of the most perplexing questions of his time, including those concerning God, creation, angelology, souls, the messiah, the millennium, hell, resurrection, and sacred literature.[32]

Keith and other Quakers were continually exposed to kabbalistic thought during their visits to Ragley to meet with van Helmont and Conway. Keith, in particular, embraced some of the ideas he found there because they offered him an answer to the seemingly theoretical gap between Christianity's professed universalism and its postulations of exclusion and damnation of those outside its community. He became particularly excited about the Kabbalah's affinity with some of his teachings, especially the view that Christ's soul was extended throughout the universe. When Keith discovered that von Rosenroth and van Helmont had already made interesting parallels between Christ and the kabbalistic figure, *Zeir Anpin*, he was delighted. In an initial letter written to von Rosenroth, Keith elaborated on the analogy:

... if the application of Sier [sic] Anpin to Christ holds, it will be of sufficient use for my point and will confirm my proposition. For I have wished that in Christ there is a certain most divine soul that is everywhere extended and that as it touches all human souls illuminates and vivifies them with its virtue, with the result that impious souls are turned back towards God and purged so that they may enjoy God by means of this most divine soul of Christ. For I know most certainly that no human soul (excepting alone that of the man Jesus Christ) is able to approach God immediately. For this reason it is necessary for us to approach God by a certain medium and by a ladder, by which medium we may enjoy God. The essence of God is exceedingly simple and, as far as his nature is concerned, remote from us.[33]

Keith's conviction that the Kabbalah confirmed some of his developing theological views inspired Conway and van Helmont. Realizing the rich potential in integrating Quaker and Kabbalah theologies, the two felt that at last they had found a practicing religious group receptive to their optimistic, all-inclusive philosophical orientations. Conway, van Helmont, and Keith explored crucial correlations between Quaker ideas and kabbalistic thought and developed creative collaboration projects, as evinced by the writings (inclusive of Conway's own treatise) that emerged during 1675–79.[34]

Conway's readings in metaphysics and other esoteric writings had prepared her for this important moment in her life. Before meeting Keith in person, she had read his work and had grasped the import of some of his innovative Christological insights. In a lengthy letter she sent to More in November 1675, Conway mentioned Keith's possible resonance with her own biblical hermeneutics, foregrounding her interest in the Kabbalah:

I am sure this new notion of G. Keiths about Christ seems farr removed from Familisme, he attributing by that more to the externall Person of our Savior, than I think any ever hath done; he was speaking of it here, for it seemed very clear to him, and he was very full of it, but I have had more thought about it since he went upon the reading his letter to you and that to Peganius (which I have also sent you a copy of) which I had not leisure to doe before, upon the perusing of which, I cannot but judge the opinion worth your serious consideration, and, I hope, you will not think your time mispent in urging such solid reasons as you may have against it in answer to what of reason and particular experience he alledges for it; his opinion, if true, would facilitate the understanding of many places in Scripture, as well as it would make better sense of the Cabbalists Soir-Aupin and Arich-Aupin.[35]

In the same letter, Conway also disclosed to More that Keith's apparent affinities with the Kabbalah were patently obvious to her, to which More reacted with his usual scorn for Keith's fantastical conceit and unwarranted enthusiasm.[36]

One appeal of kabbalistic thought to Conway was its conceptual usefulness for countering the dominant Protestant theological system of John Calvin (1509–64), one of the most powerful figures in Christian history, and whose influence in England was still felt during Conway's time. Calvin and his followers exercised the right to excommunicate those who did not conform to their doctrines, requiring everyone to subscribe publicly, on oath, to the twenty-one articles of the Christian faith. He conducted a vigilant and punitive inquisition into private morals, believing that all was done conscientiously and for the glory of God—a deity created in Calvin's image, of course. Calvin's version of predestination was built upon two of his fundamental beliefs: the sovereignty of God and the utter depravity of humanity.

For Conway, Calvinism represented everything about Christianity that she despised. For example, she considered eternal punishment of finite sins inconsistent with God's mercy and justice. As well, she considered preposterous the thought of God damning people who, through no fault of their own, had never heard of Christianity. Furthermore, with her kabbalistic leanings, Conway believed pain and suffering beneficial, and any perceived punishments from God were intelligible only within the context of eventual salvation for all. In her treatise, which I discuss in detail in the next chapter, Conway rejected Calvin's doctrine of predestination and his concept of an eternal hell while advancing the notion of universal salvation.[37]

With the lively exchanges and conversations occurring among Conway, van Helmont, and Keith, Ragley became a remarkable site for innovative theological developments in the seventeenth century. Conway's grasp of Lurianic metaphysics led her to dismiss the ontological depravity that formed the basis of Calvin's theological anthropology. She envisioned humanity as a spark of divinity that had fallen into the world of matter and was potentially capable of restoring its true divinity. Other radical thinkers of the seventeenth century who espoused millennarian orientations and dreams of perfectionism also shared this more positive view of humanity. For example, among the overlapping themes found within Gnostic, alchemical, and kabbalistic literatures was that of the role of humanity in remembering and recognizing its divine nature or its real condition. This epistemological impulse, of course, led to the different methods or forms of knowledge that aided humanity in restoring itself to its true nature.

The collaborative and creative exchanges among Conway, Keith, and van Helmont made it possible for them to recognize the potential affinities underlying these diverse forms. As Allison Coudert notes, "the alchemical concept of transmutation as a regenerative experience for both matter and the alchemist has striking similarities with the concept of restoration, or *tikkun*, elaborated by Isaac Luria; and the Hermetic vision of the alchemist as a Gnostic savior, who could redeem base matter has astonishing parallels with the incredible powers attributed to humanity in the Lurianic Kabbalah."[38] Moreover, the idea that the Kabbalist must prepare her limbs for the indwelling of the divine spirit, or *Shekhinah*, was common in kabbalistic thought, and a Kabbalist could also easily apply this idea to the notion of the inner Christ found within Quaker religiosity. Conway's ability to draw some crucial parallels between Lurianic and Quaker worldviews also rested upon the fact that both, in distinct ways, embraced the natural, experiential realm, avoiding an escapist trend symbolic of traditional mystical movements. Sanford Drob comments, "Rather than escape this world, the Kabbalists and Hasidim sought to spiritualize it, by drawing down energy from on high."[39] This *coincidentia oppositorium* in kabbalistic thought on quietism and activism in religion found ardent expression in Quaker religiosity in the seventeenth century. As I discuss below, the practical type of Quaker mysticism in England during the early seventeenth century imbued these notions with a zeal and fervor that destabilized social political conventions, bringing much adverse attention to the movement.

Unfortunately, the conceptual compatibilities that van Helmont, Conway, and Keith saw in Kabbalah theology and Quaker thought were not accepted by some of their peers. More and George Fox, in particular, intervened and succeeded in disrupting the love fest developing among the three. More, who had initially expressed genuine interest in the Kabbalah through his association with van Helmont and correspondence with von Rosenroth, became exasperated and often highly critical of the explorations at Ragley. While reaffirming his negative view of Quaker theology, More began identifying the dangers of the Kabbalah, which he felt suffered from the same faults and excess of feeling as Quakerism. He eventually concluded that the Kabbalah was too complex, flagrantly materialistic, pantheistic, and oriented toward atheism.[40] For his part, Fox became highly suspicious of van Helmont's kabbalistic views, primarily concerned that such teachings were adversely influencing Keith. Fox consequently instigated a meeting to investigate van Helmont's beliefs, which Fox rejected. These investigations, in turn, led to varied disputes among them regarding proper interpretation of the Kabbalah and to ensuing theological conflicts. Keith was eventually branded an apostate and van Helmont censured as the man responsible for a "pernicious error."[41] Due to her early death in 1679, Conway was unaware of these developments and did not witness the unfortunate demise of the collaborative efforts of her intellectual comrades.

QUAKER DEVOTION AND BODILY MATTERS

There is a lacuna in the correspondence between More and Conway during the decisive period of van Helmont and Conway's conversions to the Quakers; scholarly conjecture suggests that somewhere between 1676 and 1677, they took the decisive step and became official members of the group. According to Nicolson, in 1677, Conway began the Quaker practice of addressing everyone with the familiar "thee and "thou," regardless of social rank and standing.[42] Van Helmont's conversion was substantiated when news eventually spread among his circle of friends and family members that he had refused to move his hat in the presence of nobility, following the Quaker tradition that caused them so much persecution. In a letter to Princess Elizabeth of Bohemia (1618–80), whose family has befriended van Helmont, the Quaker Robert Barclay confirmed the news, proudly describing van Helmont's devotion to Quaker life and his transformation:

> Thy friend Helmont is here, & about 2 or 3 weeks ago found himself under a necessity so as he could not forbear with peace of conscience & without disobeying God to come under the contemptible appearance of one of us by keeping his hat upon his head & laying aside those other ceremonies which truth has obliged us to depart from & his doing so did not a little surprise thy brother & the Lord Craven with whom he had occasion to meet the other day the last of whom telling him he would write for news to thy sister Sophia, Helmont himself was willing I should prevent thy knowing it by any other hand.[43]

However, van Helmont's close friends and loved ones, fully aware of the full social, religious, and political repercussions of his joining the

Quakers, were not as enthusiastic. For instance, Leibniz, a good friend, was incredulous when he heard the news: "As for M. Helmont, I am told that he is entirely Quakerized, and that he does not bare his head when he speaks to princes. I have a hard time believing this because when I used to speak to him fairly often and familiarly eight years ago, he seemed to me entirely reasonable and since than I have esteemed him highly."[44] Leibniz's sentiment reflected his generation's undue emphasis on reason and adherence to social conformity, which was also a major concern of More in his correspondence with Conway.

Given the period as well as her position in society, Conway's conversion to the Quakers was considered a bolder and much more audacious choice than van Helmont's—her identity as a Quaker was even worse than being a female intellectual and author. This general sentiment was reflected by More, who cringed at the image of Conway belonging to a sect that symbolized all he feared and hated. In April 1677, he wrote to Conway, in response to news of her conversion: "What a peal my Lord Chancellour rang in my eares about your being turned Quaker, and what a storme I bore with be too rehearse in this letter, I told him I would either write to your Ladiship or declare by word of mouthe what he sayd when I see you."[45] According to his biographer Henry Ward, the famous scholar tried his best to alter the decision:

> It ... affected him so much at length that he receiv'd the Account of it with Tears, and labour'd all that a Faithful Friend could do, to set her right, as to her Judgment in these Matters. He both convers'd with, and wrote to these Persons, and made Remarks ... as particularly on Mr. Keith's *Immediate Revelation*. He wrote Mr. Pen a very excellent letter concerning Baptism and the Lord's Supper. And for their great leader (as most account of him) George Fox himself, he said to some; That in conversing with him, he felt himself, as it were, turned into Brass. So much did the Spirit, Crookedness of Perverseness of that Person, move and offend his Mind ... as he argued thus Occasionally with these heads of the Quakers, and exercis'd his Pen both for this Lady's, and their own Benefit; so he was not wanting in his more particular Applications to her self ... But when he saw that could not prevail, he was forced to desist; and leave that Great person to enjoy in her Extremities the Company and the Ways that she most fancied.[46]

Contemporary readers may find More's response overly dramatic or historically quaint, given our post-Enlightenment sensibilities that honor diversity, difference, and individual integrity. More's reaction to his friend's conversion is noteworthy, however, because it helps capture the full social and political significance of Conway's religious choice. Conway's decision to become a Quaker was made in an age of crises—continual social, political, and cultural upheavals—where only seven years out of a hundred were peaceful ones. This was an era that experienced ongoing religious controversies regarding orthodox and heretical teachings, with the Quakers emerging as prime exemplars of unorthodoxy. As W. K. Jordan states, "No other sect in the Civil war period was so universally hated and feared as the Quakers. Their contempt for public authority, their apparent irreverence, their disavowal of the literal truth of Holy Writ, their strange habit and stranger conduct, and extreme intolerance toward other Christian sects made them appear dangerous to civil and religious stability and aroused the concerted wrath of age disposed to deal violently with eccentric and anti-social exhibition."[47]

Conway's conversion to the Quakers also corroded More's earlier, naive assumption that Conway's interest in the Quakers was mere intellectual curiosity. Indeed, the Quakers offered Conway a new worldview, an innovative way of being in the world that helped her make sense of a set of embodied truths found in esoteric wisdom. Conway's interest in Quakers was not due solely to their emphasis on simplicity, or to their variant form of Christianity, but fundamentally on a shared sense of embodied suffering. Describing Conway, Nicolson observes, "Like frail humanity from the beginning, she reached out her groping hand to *see* and *feel* the wounds; and in the constant presence in her chamber of 'such living examples of great patience under sundry heavy exercises,' she found at length visible denial of her doubts, and living affirmation of her 'faythe'—the Word made flesh."[48] Notwithstanding Nicolson's hagiographic devotion, her comments are insightful. A woman of Conway's social and class privilege would normally empathize with the sufferings of such a marginalized group, not become a member of it. (Recall More's anguished, desperate response to Conway's decision.)

Conway's fascination with mystical lore and her desire for a profound experience of the divine led her to a decision that few women or men of her social standing would take upon themselves. Consider, for example, Elizabeth of Bohemia, or Princess of Palatine, an acquaintance of both Conway and van Helmont, who was also exposed to Quaker thought. While Elizabeth found some Quaker ideas interesting, and their conversions fascinating, she chose not to give up her social privileges and honor, as did Conway. In response to Barclay, who began discussing with her the value of Conway's conversion, Elizabeth replied: "I cannot submit unto the opinion or practise of any other, thought I grant that they have more light than myself. The Countesse of Conway [sic] doth well to go the way that she thinks best, but I shold not doe well to follow her, unless I had the same conviction, neither did it ever enter into my thoughts to do so."[49] The responses from both More and Elizabeth illustrate the degree of Conway's passionate, explorative spirit and independence of thought—rare, unexpected, and undesirable qualities associated with women of the time.

Conway's empathetic, daring mystical reasoning enabled her to make a vital connection between her own bodily suffering and the suffering of those moved by love toward divine goodness:

> The weight of my affliction lies so very heavy upon me, that it is incredible how very seldom I can endure anyone in my chamber, but I find them so still and very serious, that the company of such of them as I have hitherto seene, will be acceptable to me, as long as I am capable of enjoying any; the particular acquaintance with such living examples of great patience under sundry heavy exercises, both of bodily sicknesse and other calamitys (as some of them have related to me) I find begetts a more lively fayth and uninterrupted desire of approaching to such a behavior in like exigencyes, than the most learned and Rhetorical discourses of resignation can doe, though such also are good and profitable in their season.[50]

Conway recognized among the Friends a type of profound faith that was not mere common intellectual assent to propositional truths; in their lives, she grasped and appreciated a modality or a way of being in the world, namely, a full (embodied) commitment to illuminating goodness that confronted one, awakening one to transformative action in the world.

The tales of the sufferings and degradation of Quaker women in English prisons moved the feeble, bedridden Conway to action. During her last years, she unceasingly advocated for the Quakers, who were persecuted and imprisoned for their stance against social conventions. Conway's devotion to her new "family" even extended to the point of asking her husband to intervene on their behalf. While willing to help his wife, Lord Conway remained hostile toward the Quakers. In one letter written in October 1678, several years after her conversion, Lord Conway both acknowledged that he continued to help Quakers out of devotion to her and suggested that they deserved their imprisonment and harassment:

All the Quaker wives whose husbands I acquainted you formerly were in prison, are at this instant in the House waiting for me because Mr. Lovell the Chancellor hath appointed this day to give me an answer about them. All the matter is, I must pay the Fees my selfe, yet I hope to have them released before night, and what service soever I can doe you I shall always doe it, but I finde them to be a senselesse, wilful, ridiculous generation of people, rather to be pitied then envyed.[51]

Rather than arguing or contending with him, Conway sent her husband some Quaker books, hoping the literature itself would help him understand why she was genuinely devoted to this group. Lord Conway's travels and business affairs kept him very busy and absent from Ragley for extended periods, so he could only despair from afar of his wife's intimate relationship with the Quakers. In another letter written several months later, Conway's husband continued to reveal his distaste for his wife's group of friends: "He [Frank Parson, a servant of the Conways] tells me that you order'd him to returne me thanks for my kindnesse to your friends in the truth. If you reckon them all so that are in that profession I assure you have a pack of as arrant knaves to your friends as any I know."[52]

Conway's act of solidarity with the Quakers in the seventeenth century—via her sense of shared bodily suffering—resonates with profound conceptual and historical importance. For example, Conway's ability to see certain connections between the bodily suffering of two classes of people draws attention to the potentially emancipatory nature of her mystical religiosity in blurring, even dissolving, traditional lines and divisions between respectable and disrespectable philosophies and religious systems, between high and low culture, and between politics and faith. Additionally, Conway's keen sense of taking suffering seriously reveals an important theoretical notion, which, while undeveloped in Conway's time, has become a standard feature in current feminist and postcolonial theories: the body matters. In Conway's encounters with the Quakers, the body is transformed into a rich symbolic discursive site delineating the impossibility of eluding materiality when assessing the necessary interconnections among religion, philosophy, society, class, gender, and politics. Put another way, Conway's reflective relationship to her infirmed female body allowed her to understand and share in the extended effects of unjust suffering by collective bodies that were bound and classified together as Friends—those deemed enemies of the state. In writing to More, she observed: "They have been and are a suffering people and are taught from the consolation [that] has been experimentally felt by them under their great tryals to administer comfort upon occasion to others in great distresse, and as Solomon sayes, a word in due season is like apples of gold in pictures of silver."[53] Moreover, in Conway's letters, in the meals shared among the various visitors at her home, and in the salons and lengthy conversations and occurring among Kabbalists, Platonists, and Quakers, the trope of the "body" functions to augment the politics of class, of religion, of gender, of truth—all variables Foucault would identify as an episteme with its own set of power/knowledge discourse.

Conway embraced a religious group whose intimations of embodied piety preshadowed later, more explicit views of bodily integrity that have been celebrated so much in twentieth-century feminist and liberationist discourses. Fox and Friends offered a discursive politics of the body (involving many layers of semiotic signification) that was revolutionary in its deployment. Notably, Friends did not formulate a coherent political theory, as did many of their seventeenth-century contemporaries (e.g., Thomas Hobbes, John Locke, and James Harrington); rather, they heralded a new manner of understanding and inhabiting the integrity of the body in the world—in word, in action, and in dress. Early Quakers rejected the laws of the land and advocated a different authorial presence of divinity in people's bodies and lives, believing they were emulating Jesus as described in the Gospel accounts.

One plausible reading of the Quakers' despised bodies is that they represent a variant discourse of knowledge in early modern literature, presenting disruptive fissures to the dominant models of religious and social control, authority, and reasoning. Consider, for example, the revolutionary ambiance in which the Quakers originated, and that the movement was very much a creature of its age, part of the radicalism and enthusiasm of the revolutionary years.[54] Quaker bodies threatened civil society's privileges and honors, forms of power, and its established social order, generating instinctively hostility to their practices and ideals. Quaker women and men in the seventeenth century became easy targets for hostile, reactionary fear in the same way black bodies were targeted during the various attempts to integrate schools and other public institutions during the twentieth-century civil rights movement in North America. During Conway's time, the justices belonging to the country nobility and the priests of the established Church were the ones who initiated much of the persecution of Friends. Fox was imprisoned in Nottingham for some time in 1649 and put in the stocks at Mansfield Woodhouse shortly after his release for speaking in church. He spent a year in Derby jail for blasphemy and for refusing to serve in the parliamentary army.[55] Within fifteen years after his first preaching trip, four thousand Quakers were imprisoned, thirty-three had died in England from prison abuses, and three were hung in North America.

Within this context, there emerged the group's collective affirmation of its truths, or the production of a distinct body of Friends' literature such as the memoir, the journal, and the confessional, which became innovative means for expressing the religious life. Quakers' "publishers of truth" were subject to persecution almost from the beginning.[56] Furthermore, a body of laws arose, preventing Friends from experiencing the full freedoms extended to other citizens. For example, the Conventicle Act in 1664 forbade the unauthorized meeting of more than five persons. The Blasphemy Act of 1650 asserted that persons affirming themselves or any creatures to be God, or God's equal, or affirming that the true God dwells in the human and nowhere else, were liable for imprisonment. It was not until the Toleration Act of 1689 that Quakers were allowed to meet and worship in comparative peace.

EMBODIED MYSTICISM, PHILOSOPHY, AND DIVINIZED, POLITICIZED BODIES

Viewing the Quaker body as a discursive, political text in seventeenth-century England stretches our imagination to reconsider an important aim of contemporary analyses of the body: considering how bodies think and how thought is embodied in the Western intellectual heritage. One major concern here is that conceptualizations of the body in humanistic thinking have necessitated its omission, exclusion, or repression, even while (ironically) depending on its very condition as an insuperable limit to discourses of knowledge, language, and thought. In his essay, "Corpus," Jean-Luc Nancy alludes to this problem by suggesting that there has never been any "body" in philosophy. Nancy considers a perennial problem in philosophic writing on the body since Descartes: the demand of philosophies, over time, that have enabled the separation of mind and body. Nancy attempts to demonstrate the vexed relationship that philosophical—and consequent literary and theoretical—writings have had to the body. Dating as far back as Plato's allegory of the cave, this strain of thought has issued metaphysical opposites—inside/outside; the being itself of the sign, the sign of itself—that have perpetuated this tendency. Nancy writes:

Literature mimes the body, or makes the body mime a signification (social, psychology, historical, heroic, etc.), or mimes itself as body. In this way, in all these ways at once, sense always comes back to the book as such, that is, to literature itself, but the book is never there: it has never abolished itself in its pure presence, it has not absorbed the sign sense, nor sense into the sign. The body of the book, which should be the body of bodies, is there without being there. Literature, and with it, once again, the relationship between literature and philosophy, is a long sequel to the mystery of the Incarnation, a long explication of it, a long implication within it.[57]

An illuminating feature of Nancy's argument is his insistence on the inescapable materiality of the body (of sensate-ness) that precedes (yet is the very condition for) any theory of the body. For Nancy, bodies resist, have weight, extension—bodies experience themselves, are experienced not as bodies as incarnations of spirit, but as bodies that are given, there. A body is the determination of something like an instance of immediate knowledge—a contradiction in terms, constituting philosophy's objection to the body. In other words, discourse on the body helps raise a disconcerting truth regarding the body—we can never escape "it," yet we (theorists) constantly elude it in our representative efforts or significations. In a dominant Western trajectory, our systems of thought have unceasing signified the body, assigning signs to it; while, paradoxically, body can only do this by allowing itself to be brought back to its own thinking matter, to the very place from which it thoughtlessly springs. In this context, empirical selves (physical, moral, gendered, classed, racialized, violated, suffering bodies) fail to go beyond the illusory desires of transcendental, categorical, linguistically constructed selves. In short, bodies' materiality can never be fully recovered or contained in thought about the body. As Nancy suggests,

A swallowed, unspoken word, not choked back, not retracted, but swallowed in the stolen instant of being spoken, swallowed with this bare taste of saliva, barely foaming, barely viscous, a distinct dissolution, impregnation without the beginning of a blandness where what is given in the taste of the swallowed word, washed away before being uttered. This savor is not savoir, whatever the etymological link.[58]

Another aspect of Nancy's analysis that I find intriguing is his suggestion that in embodied theological discourse, the mysterious fluid and dynamic intimations of body and sense are vital forces that are felt throughout an individual body as well as in society. If one agrees with Nancy's assertion that thought does not belong to the order of knowledge, then it may not be impossible to say that the body thinks and, consequently, to further argue that thought is itself a body. This amounts to saying "only that thought is here taken back to 'matter,' to its matter—thought is itself this renewal that does not come back, but that comes, properly speaking, to this existence—posited, suspended, confined in this very block, this network of tissues, bones, minerals, and fluids out of which it does not go, because, if it did exit, it would no longer think."[59] Nancy further suggests that, in turn, politics represents the same phenomenon, the same endless explication of mystery. As a body of forces, as a body of love, as a sovereign body, " 'body' is both sense and the sign of its own sense—but as soon as it is the one, it loses the other. . . . Sign of itself and being-itself of the sign: such is the double formula of the body in all its states, in all its possibilities."[60]

Nancy's provocative ideas lead me to consider a much more expansive view of the material value of Quaker religiosity for Conway: their embodied mysticism. For early Quakers, a major emphasis was in knowing the divine experimentally, not merely through abstract theories or signification. Fox and Friends were adamant about not needing seductive theories or misleading systematic theology (creeds, articles of faith, or catechism). They sought one shelter only, and that was a mutuality of love experienced between God and humanity on earth. Distinguishing between the historical figure of Christ, who had died, and the voice of the living, vital Christ within, Fox taught that in each individual there was a light, that of the divine, sufficient to make the individual one with God, if one turned it toward God, its source.

These English Quakers were not systematic theologians, so this "Inner light" was variously described as the "Christ within" every person, an impersonal force, the Holy Spirit, or the Father.[61] For many Quakers, the "Inner light" represented the power of divinity (re)vitalizing the person who embodied an intimate and immediate experience of divine transformation. Granted, in some contexts, the "Inner light" seemed to reflect Puritan influence—associated with the terror of sin well as the beauty of divine love. In these cases, it symbolized an experience of transformation in which the self, entirely liberated from bondage of sin and taint of self-will, entered into a new state of freedom.[62] Experiencing the light within simultaneously brought the individual to judgment before God and transformed her into a vessel and instrument of God's power in its dealings with humanity. As Robert Fouke asserts, in such cases the "Inner light" was distinguished

from subjective inclinations of any kind, from mental power or intelligence, and from conscience.[63]

A much more provocative understanding of the "Inner light"
was found in the accounts of those Quakers who believed they were
divine, embodying truths that could not be contained or held by human control. With these assumptions, Friends enacted a radical truth
into the world: the divinized, politicized body—and in the provocative sense to which Nancy alludes. The trembling or quaking that
earned them their name was a sign of divine possession for Quakers,
and a sign of terror signalizing the dismantling of the social order for
others. In *The Irreligion of the Quakers*, Higgins, a contemporary critic
described this behavior as strange, bizarre phenomenon:

> Though their speakings be a very chaos of words and errors, yet
> very often while they are speaking, so strange is the effect of them
> in their unblest followers, that many of them, sometimes men, but
> more frequently women and children, fall into quaking
> fits. . . . While the agony of the fit is upon them their lips quiver,
> their flesh and joints tremble, their bellies swell as though blown
> up with wind, they foam at the mouth, and sometimes purge as
> if they had taken physic.[64]

One easy, oversimplified interpretation of this phenomenon is that the
mystery of the incarnation cannot be contained in rational understanding; however, one could go as far as to suggest, in light of Nancy's
thesis, that here we see an enactment of the body of forces, of the body
of love in religious discourse in which both the sense and the sign of
its own sense move between and among the other. As various Quakers' experiences revealed in the seventeenth century, in all its states, in
all its possibilities, the body of love—or, the divinized, politicized
body—refuses a static ontology, an essence that is determinable and
controllable by others.

A variant of this bodily mysticism was the belief in the human
capacity to transcend sin, as evinced in the testimonies of Quaker women
who maintained they experienced painless childbirth, a clear indication
that they had returned to a prelaspsarian state.[65] Fox himself exemplified this radical notion most supremely, as suggested in his theological
description of celestial adoption or celestial inhabitation:

> Now I was come up in the spirit through the Flaming Sword, into
> the Paradise of God. All things were new; and all the creation
> gave unto me another smell than before, beyond what words can

utter. I knew nothing but pureness, and innocency, and righteous-
ness; being renewed into the image of God by Christ Jesus, to the
state of Adam, which he was in before he fell. The creation was
opened to me, and it was showed me how all things had their
names given them according to their nature and virtue.[66]

Out of his dissatisfaction with names as substitutes for experience, Fox
began a search for divinity he could know "experimentally," inexhaust-
ibly, apart from its purported knowledge within the oppressive theoretical discourse of Christian orthodoxy. This search for a fuller, different
model of divine knowledge constituted the basis of an existential revolution in religion, of which the Quakers remain the most extreme example in the seventeenth century. Such emphasis on an experiential,
bodily form of knowledge also shares some affinity with the second-
century Gnostics, who advocated that individuals could gain the necessary knowledge for salvation through their own efforts and without the
theological intervention of the emerging Orthodox Church.

Quakers' embodied mysticism eventually led to the practice of
the group's keeping silence before God: a notion at the center of Quaker
corporate life. The efficacious role of the Friends meeting for worship
and testimonies was its power to induce the Light of God to flood into
the conscious mind. Here again the importance and integrity of the
body is key. Quakers were individuals who experienced divinity for
the purpose of embodying God's will and carrying it out in the world
around them. The ultimate goal of feeling the presence was not to feel
good, but to be/do good. Union with divinity was not an end in and
of itself; it was not even truly experienced if the life the human lived
did not exemplify divine nature. Thus, the Friends that Conway met
at Ragley were appealing to her because they embodied the presence
of divinity—for them, the living incarnation. They tapped afresh the
vital forces in (and symbolic power of) Christianity and entered a new
modality, which they enacted uncompromisingly, inviting all people
to share in it. For these early Quakers, Christianity ceased to be a set
of forms and notions that left the moral life practically untouched;
rather, it was a new type of firsthand experience of divine love and
goodness. With several other radical sects of the seventeenth century,
the Quakers expressed a religiosity that brought forceful experience to
its adherents.

Unlike many others, who expended their new energy in personal
piety expressed in sanctioned religious forms, the Quakers' new experiences and devotion were channeled into new patterns of life, into novel
ways of being human and embodying truth that had monumental social

and cultural ramifications. For example, more so than most other Protestant sects, Quakers offered women much more independence in
matters of worship and religious leadership.[67] Growing out of discon-
tent with its Puritan roots, the early movement, spreading in southern
and eastern Europe around 1655, was advanced not only by men but
also by women preachers: Anne Blaykling, Mary Fisher, Dorothy
Waugh, Jane Waugh, and Mary Pennington. Some of these women
became traveling preachers, bearing the Quaker message not only all
over England, but also as far as the Ottoman Empire. Under the leadership of Fox, separate meetinghouses were established, administered,
and attended solely by women throughout England.[68]

The intensity with which the Quakers enacted their practical
mysticism appealed to Conway's own passionate desire to understand
the mysterious nature of embodied divinity, which she felt in her own
selfhood. Whether reading books, listening to sermons, entering into
cultural debates and theological controversies, or collaborating on
scholarly projects, Conway and her various friends at Ragley were
intent on one thing: experiencing divinity. For Conway, the quest for
an authentic, vital experience of divinity culminated in her formal
treatise, *The Principles*, which incorporated both Quaker sensibilities
and Kabbalah doctrines.

CHAPTER 3

Conway, Descartes, and the New Mechanical Science

> Nature is not simply an organic body like a clock, which has no vital principle of motion in it; but it is a living body which has life and perception, which are much more exalted than a mere mechanism or a mechanical motion.
>
> —Anne Conway, *The Principles*

Throughout much of its history up to the present day, modern science has been primarily associated with methodological observation, experimentation, and inductive reasoning. However, devotion to this model of scientific inquiry has distorted its humble beginnings in the early modern period—during the rise and establishment of English science, or the new philosophy, as it was called at that time, there were a plurality of theoretical positions. With the aid of new historical studies of the last forty years, scholars have reassessed the emergence of scientific inquiry in seventeenth-century England, drawing closer attention to these myriad approaches—especially the importance of religion—to initial investigations of nature. The discussions and debates between Conway and her contemporaries occurred during this formative period, where religious, philosophical, and scientific ideas were often integrated into epistemological models, legitimizing one or another particular investigation of nature.[1] Recent investigations also challenge a standard view of the nineteenth century that still holds sway in many quarters, that is, that science advanced and replaced religion rather quickly. As the writings and conversations engaging Conway suggest, most forms of natural knowledge were intimately and inseparably linked to, and inspired by, particular forms of religious belief and practice.

EMERGENCE OF EXPERIMENTAL PHILOSOPHY

Since the translation of Aristotle's works from Arabic into Latin in the thirteenth century, Aristotelianism had served as the primary conceptual framework for observing the natural world. During the early part of the seventeenth century, some natural philosophers began constructing a new paradigm to replace Aristotelian scientific explanations, which they considered bankrupt in light of the skeptical crisis, the Copernican revolution, the Reformation, and the Renaissance revival of ancient philosophies of nature.[2] Although Aristotelian natural philosophers in the mid-seventeenth century persisted in explaining the observable facts of nature in terms of the intermixing of the four elements, substantial forms, and final causation, the new experimental scientists found these explanations lacking in empirical validity. Rejecting the "antiquities and citations of authors," and insisting that scientists employ methodical observation, experimentation, and inductive reasoning, figures like Francis Bacon (1561–1626) helped lay the foundation for a new turn to direct perception—to the things themselves—as the basis of all knowledge.[3] In 1661, Joseph Glanville, echoing a Baconian sentiment, epitomized these thinkers' objections to Aristotelianism: it was merely verbal, it did not give a satisfactory account of phenomenon, and it did not lead to discoveries for "the use of common life."[4] By the late seventeenth century, Bacon was heralded as the hero of a new world of discovery, his name epitomizing cooperative empirical philosophy.

In his 1664 work, *Experimental Philosophy*, Henry Power (1623–68) articulated a general view shared by most natural philosophers and physicians, that is, that the divine Artisan made this world to be studied by humanity. Power favored the new mechanical philosophy because it explained Christians' responsibility to God and revealed the divine plan for the universe. Keeping in mind the homage due to God, Power eagerly embraced a new era that signaled the decline of the Aristotelian epistemological model.

These are the days that must lay a new Foundation of a more magnificent Philosophy, never to be overthrown, that will Empirically and Sensibily canvass the *Phaenomena* of Nature, deducing the Causes of things from such Originals in Nature as we observe are producible by Art, and the infallible demonstration of Mechanicsk: and certainly, this is the way, and no other, to build a true and permanent Philosophy. . . . And to speak yet more close to the point, I think it is no Rhetorication to say That all things are Artificial, for Nature it self is nothing else but the Art of God. Then, certainly, to find the various turnings and mysterious process of this divine Art, in the management of this great machine of the World, must needs be the proper Office and onely the Experimental and Mechanical Philosopher.[5]

At the most abstract level, mechanistic science introduced a new metaphysics that endowed the natural order with only one kind of entity: matter. Assuming that all natural phenomena could be explained in terms of simple observations of matter in motion, mechanical philosophers constructed a physics of the universe in which planets were material objects whose motions in space were described in mathematical form. Mechanistic science described a homogeneous universe, all the parts of which were governed by the same laws of nature. To help advance their theories, many mechanists appealed to atomism, which, since its revival in the late sixteenth century, had become a primary epistemological framework for those observing natural processes. The atomistic model provided easy, systematic, and reliable explanations for understanding the impact of matter with matter, or the causality determining the movement of gross bodies. As did the ancient atomists, so the new atomists explained observable phenomena on the basis of the size, shape, and motion of particles of matter.

Despite differences in politics, nationality, or theological convictions, thinkers such as Isaac Beeckman (1588–1637), Marin Mersenne (1588–1648), Thomas Hobbes (1588–1679), Pierre Gassendi (1592–1655), and Rene Descartes (1596–1650) defended the mechanical philosophy against an Aristotelian metaphysics of matter, form, and privation; they also rejected the Neoplatonically inspired animistic philosophies of the Renaissance.[6] In presuming that all natural phenomena can be explained in terms of matter and motion alone, and that there is no action at a distance, mechanical philosophers departed from traditional philosophies of nature, which had endowed matter with various kinds of activity. In their various writings describing the ultimate components of the world (matter and motion), seventeenth-century natural philosophers also advanced the doctrine of primary and secondary qualities. For most, all phenomena in the natural world were explained in terms of the properties of matter alone, so the question of which properties are essential to matter became extremely important. Many shared the perspective that material bodies possessed only a few primary qualities, and that the observed qualities of bodies actually resulted from the interaction of the primary qualities with our sense organs. In numerous ways, and with varying degrees of emphasis, natural philosophers mechanized the natural world and human perception, declaring that qualities are subjective and relative to the human perceiver.

For many of its advocates, mechanism was compatible with developments in astronomy, the science of motion, and physiology. For example, Descartes considered William Harvey's proof for the circulation of blood "much easier to conceive" if understood in mechanical terms.[7] Harvey's success in applying Descartes' mechanical model to the phenomenon of blood circulation inspired other physiologists to apply it to their descriptions of other bodily functions, such as digestion and metabolism. These attempts ultimately failed since the phenomena physiologists tried to explain involved chemical processes that were unknown at the time and could not be described solely in mechanical terms.

The mechanical worldview arose out of certain cultural sensibilities favoring the vital interconnections among epistemology, theology, cosmology, morality, and politics. These assumptions caused most individuals to be wary of any conception of the world that would desacralize it and lead to all forms of social disorder. As Michael Hunter asserts, "for many, the most important social corollary of intellectual life was the way it informed conduct. It was widely believed that the fabric of society depended on a philosophical and theological consensus, and hence unorthodox viewpoints which seemed to undermine this and to encourage immoral attitudes were regarded with alarm."[8] With the possible exception of Hobbes and his followers, the majority of mechanical thinkers avoided a materialist atheism traditionally associated with Epicurean atomism. Embracing their roles as the new cosmological artisans, seventeenth-century mechanists often posited God as the source of motion in the world that necessarily lies outside of the natural, material realm. Various systems featured God as an absolute fixture; elaborate treatises often contained specific sections on the existence of God, the nature of God's providential relationship to humanity, and the doctrine of the immortal human soul. The basic drive to retain some form of theism in a mechanistic universe subsequently led many thinkers to reject the notion of active matter. According to such logic, a conception of nature as self-moving possibly could lead to an explanation of the world that did not warrant an appeal to God or to the supernatural. One could avoid such danger if one conceives matter as naturally inert and able to produce its effects only by mechanical impact.

As the various forms of mechanistic science increased in popularity, many fundamental philosophical and theological truths (e.g., freedom of the will, the incorporeality of the soul, and the doctrine of biblical creation) became the focus of heated debates. For example, Hobbes' appropriation of Epicurean atomism as a metaphysical first principle led him to reject traditional belief in freedom of the will. With his atomistic theory, Hobbes assessed mind based on its sensory contents and defined knowledge as a process of tracing the objects of perception back to the motion of bodies in space.[9] If, as Hobbes argued, all is matter in motion—even thought—then antecedent physical motions determine our choices; hence, freedom of the will is an illusion. The methodological orientations and epistemic assumptions of mechanism also dethroned traditional metaphysics, calling it into question. Also known as first philosophy, metaphysics in the seventeenth century was primarily concerned with the nature and existence of God, mind, and body, and with specific relationships between mind and body. Descartes' original title for *The Meditation on First Philosophy* was *The Metaphysics*—the change of title perhaps illustrating the pejorative force given to the old metaphysics. Yet, that Descartes could alter the title indicates the interchangeability of the terms. With its tainted association with scholasticism, the term metaphysics eventually signified obscure and meaningless speech. Hobbes derisively described metaphysicians' use of insignificant speech. Bacon retained the term, but assigned it to the study of form redefined as the mechanical laws governing the interaction of bodies.[10]

DESCARTES' MECHANICAL PHILOSOPHY

Despite mechanism's widening spheres of influence and applicability, as well as the general theological orientation held by most of its advocates, some critics believed it was dangerous and likely to disrupt the harmony of established society. These critics, pointing to the development of Hobbesian materialism and to Spinoza's identification of God with nature, asserted that mechanism, in whatever variety, was a potential threat to the belief in the incorporeal soul, and, by extension, to traditional theism. Other astute observers, like Conway, targeted Descartes, warning that the dualistic features supporting his mechanistic worldview could possibly lead to a desacralized world in which love and empathy for all forms of nature were conspicuously absent. The focus on Descartes was not unwarranted, for he was a pioneer of mechanical philosophy and a leading practitioner of mathematics and other scientific endeavors such as optics, anatomy, and physiology. As a practicing scientist and a metaphysician, Descartes' views on nature were full of unresolved tensions and ambiguities—"continually in process, contested and negotiated during his life and after his death."[11]

In *The World* (or *Treatise on Light*), written in 1629–33, but not published during his lifetime, Descartes began conceptualizing a mechanistic worldview. Descartes opened *The World* with a full exposition of his views on light, but beginning with chapter six, he began his general analysis of nature. Appealing neither to experience nor to existing theories, Descartes constructed a theoretical model of nature constituted by various elements that one could readily imagine. He envisioned matter as a "real, perfectly solid body uniformly filling the entire length, breadth, and depth of this huge space," and characterized the differences of matter as "consisting in the differences of motion God gives to its parts."[12] In his theoretical construction, Descartes identified three primary elements: God, the creator and conserver, who always acts in the same way; the material aspect of concrete extension; and the formal aspect or laws of movement.

> Note . . . that by 'nature' here I do not mean some goddess or any other sort of imaginary power. Rather, I am using this word to signify matter itself, in so far as I am considering it taken together with all the qualities I have attributed to it, and under the condition that God continues to preserve it in the same way that he created it. For it follows of necessity, from the mere fact that he continues thus to conserve it, that there must be many changes in its parts which cannot, it seems to me, properly be attributed to the action of God (because that action never changes), and which therefore I attribute to nature. The rules by which these changes take place I call the 'laws of nature.'[13]

In this early construction of nature, Descartes did not make any claims regarding the essence of things, except to say that it was not necessary for them to have real qualities. At this juncture, he merely provided a theoretical model for understanding matter in motion. Later, in *The Meditations* (1641) and *The Principles of Philosophy* (1644), Descartes sought a metaphysical legitimacy for his natural philosophy that was not present in *The World*. Descartes then believed that he had the epistemological grounds for claiming that the world was, as he understood it to be, that is, he could form a clear and distinct idea of the essence of matter: "I now know that even bodies are not strictly perceived by the sense or the faculty of imagination but the intellect alone, and that this perception derives not from their being touched or seen but from their being understood."[14] This claim to a priori, certain knowledge constituted, in part, Descartes' response to the skeptical challenge of his day. Part of his task involved demonstrating mathematical truths (or eternal truths) that he believed were created by God.[15]

The complexity and vastness of Descartes' complete views on nature cannot be fully addressed here; however, two important elements of his thought are especially relevant to my discussion about Conway in this chapter. The first has to do with Descartes' mature physics, where he outlined matter as an extended body that was in motion; the second refers to Descartes' bold assertion that mind and matter were utterly distinct and incompatible. With reference to the former, Descartes' general physics can be described very briefly. As a mechanist, Descartes typically posited the universe as consisting of matter in motion. After introducing motion into matter (or extended substance), Descartes divided matter up into bodies that have primary modes: shape and motion. In Part II of *The Principles of Philosophy*, Descartes discussed the fundamental interactions of these bodies within his system, speaking of the conservation of motion or force and three laws of nature that governed the behavior of bodies. Once in motion, he asserted, bodies constantly collided with one another.[16] The second point requires a bit more detail. In establishing knowledge on clear and distinct ideas, Descartes proposed the coexistence of two independent substances and introduced an irreducible dualism within his system: thought and extension (where the essence of mind was thought and that of body was extension). For Descartes, mechanical causation sufficiently explained activity of phenomena in *res extensa*, but it did not account for what lay in the realm of *res cogitans* (reason and free will). This general distinction was further complicated by Descartes' epistemological efforts in his *Meditations*. In searching for that which can be known indubitably, Descartes finally rested upon the *cogito*— one could doubt the existence of anything except for the thinking mind that experienced the doubt.[17] Descartes thus identified the "I" that exists with mind and distinguished it from the unthinking, extended body, which we perceive through our unreliable senses.

Despite the initial challenges of some of his contemporaries (Gassendi, for example), Descartes' dualism became immensely influential, and received favorable responses from both atomists and their theological enemies.[18] On the one hand, the atomists were attuned to Descartes' explanation of natural phenomena through the dominant metaphor of motion, as well as his theory of the emergence of the cosmos through the jostling of corpuscles. On the other hand, Descartes' reflections on the unique activity of *res cogitans* pacified some theists. For example, Descartes' presupposition of free will helped him establish the existence of God: "It is only in the will, or freedom of choice, which I experience within me to be so great that the idea of any greater faculty is beyond my grasp; so much that it is above all in virtue of the will that I understand myself to bear in some way the image and likeness of God."[19] Above all, the theists embraced Descartes' ingenious argument that carefully circumscribed God's role in natural philosophy. According to Descartes' reasoning, the idea of a deity who is eternal, infinite, immutable, omniscient and omnipotent logically leads to the assumption that God actually exists: "It is manifest by the natural light that there must be at least much "reality" in the efficient and total cause as in the effect of that cause."[20] Since, for Descartes, the cause of the idea of God could not lie in imperfect, limited humans, there must be a God actually existing who causes the idea of God in our minds. Moreover, a good God would not deceive us through appearances into believing in a material universe that does not exist.[21] It is important to note that even with such theistic assertions, Descartes made it clear that the material world was governed by mechanical laws and not by final or formal causes. With his mechanistic theory, Descartes specified which things existed in the world and the means by which they interacted.

Descartes' mechanism even extended into the realm of physiology; in 1664, he wrote one of the first scientific treatises of mechanistic physiology, *Trait de l'homme*, which was published after his death. In it, Descartes used machine metaphors (pumps, valves, and a host of other machines) to help explain the living organism, suggesting that one had only to consider the ingenious machines found in the royal gardens, some of which play musical instruments and others uttered words, to be convinced that the activities of the human organs were similarly caused. In his system, the human body, with its marvelous intricacy of design, was a machine with a difference—it had a mind attached. Moreover, aside from humanity, everything in the cosmos consisted entirely of inert, passive matter; whatever movements or actions material bodies experienced were simply the result of matter in motion.

Due, in large part, to Conway's early mentor, More, who was instrumental in introducing Descartes' ideas to England, Descartes' theory of matter exerted considerable influence on emerging perspectives regarding nature. More first became fascinated with Descartes' theories in the mid-1640s at Christ's College, and, in 1648, the two began corresponding. Professing admiration for Descartes' "sublime and subtil Mechanick," More looked upon Descartes as a "man more truly inspired in the knowledge of Nature than any that have professed themselves so these sixteen hundred years."[22] More believed Descartes' mechanical philosophy was a revival of the science of Moses, contending that the three kinds of matter to which Descartes pointed were also found in the Genesis creation account.[23] Furthermore, More felt that the systematic coherence of Cartesian science fit well with his Platonist project of establishing a universal synthesis of knowledge. In a letter to Descartes, he stated, "That which enravishes me most is that we both setting out from the same lists, though taking several wayes, the one travelling in the lower road of Democritisme, amidst the thick dust of Atoms and flying particles of Matter; the other tracing it over the high and aeiry Hills of Platonisme, in that more thin and subtil Region of Immateriality, meeting together notwithstanding at last."[24]

More's initial enthusiasm eventually lessened, however, as he perceived undesirable elements within Descartes' mechanistic metaphysics. At different times and in myriad ways, More began objecting to Descartes' mechanism, even while retaining important elements of it.[25] For example, while accepting the Cartesian concept of dead stupid matter and the dualism between matter and spirit, More and fellow Platonist Ralph Cudworth attempted to bridge the ontological gap by retaining the world's vegetative character. In positing the essential vegetative constitution of nature, they held a moderate position between two extremes: (1) the dead mechanical cosmos of the mechanists and (2) the animal-like world of the Civil War pantheists (who saw God as active and immanent in every material thing) and enthusiasts (who fanatically gave into all forms of religious passion).[26] More and Cudworth also helped advance a managerial model of nature inaugurated by John Evelyn (1620–1706), the English diarist and founding member of the Royal Society, by adapting the older organic philosophy to the new social and commercial demands of preindustrial capitalism.

Influenced by the profound changes occurring in the religious, social, and political systems of her period, Conway also participated in the theoretical debates about the "nature" of nature generated by Descartes, More, and others. She specifically addressed some of the tensions and unresolved problems she saw in Descartes' system, conceiving *The Principles of the Most Ancient and Modern Philosophy* as a major philosophical challenge to Cartesianism. In a key passage, she declared:

Let no one object that this philosophy is nothing but Cartesianism or Hobbesianism in a new guise. First, Cartesian philosophy claims that body is merely dead mass, which not only lacks life and perception of any kind but is also utterly incapable of either for all eternity. This great error must be imputed to all those who say that body and spirit are contrary things and unable to change into one another, thereby denying bodies all life and perception. This is completely contrary to the fundamentals of our philosophy. On this account it is so far from being Cartesianism in a new guise that it can more truly be called anti-Cartesianism because of its fundamental principles.[27]

Distinguishing her theoretical perspective from Descartes and other notable male thinkers of her day, Conway employed other forms of knowledge that were not readily accepted by the leading mechanists. She audaciously challenged the notion of "dead matter," inherent in Descartes' mechanist model, preferring to focus on the inner life of sentient organisms. In addressing Descartes' great error, Conway constructed an alternative understanding of "nature" in all its myriad complexity. In the process, she advanced in a unique style the constellation of ideas that were circulating among a small circle of seventeenth-century vitalists, including her devoted friend, van Helmont, his father, Jean Baptiste van Helmont, and Leibniz.[28] In this context, Conway's *Principles* may be viewed as an invaluable cultural artifact of the early modern period, depicting Conway as a high Renaissance thinker who keenly integrated occult knowledge, alchemy, ancient wisdom, and the new mode of organizing reason, or "science" represented by the mechanists.[29] In it, she introduced a conceptualization of "processional nature" that is measured and authorized by the worth of ancient and marginalized wisdoms. The result is a unique Christian cosmology or mystical naturalism that affirms a continuum of "life-affirming impulses" stretching from God through the most inconspicuous minutiae of perceived materiality.

A MYSTICAL NATURALISM:
AN OVERVIEW OF CONWAY'S COSMOLOGY

Conway began her cosmological construction by identifying three orders of being: God, Christ or Logos, and the rest of creation. These distinct dimensions of reality were constituted by a radical relationality, variously justified by both modern and ancient forms of knowledge. Conway elaborated on this unique relationality by first describing the essential nature of God, who was distinct from God's creatures, but not separated from them. She depicted divinity as the highest good, characterized with traditional divine attributes: infinitely wise, omnipotent, omniscient, and perfect. A principle of likeness linked God and creation. Since, for Conway, God was good and just, so, too, was creation. As well, all three substances shared characteristics—they all contained spirit, which accounted for the relatedness among them. For Conway, deity was present in everything—most closely and intimately, and in the highest degree. Yet Conway carefully noted that the creatures of God were not parts of God or changeable into God; nor was God changeable into them.

In a move reflective of scholastic rationalism, Conway also maintained God's immutability. According to this reasoning, any change in God implied imperfection in the divine essence and the logical existence of another being who could be greater than God. Conway thus wrote, "Now there is no greater being than God, and [he] cannot improve or be made better in any way, much less decrease, which would imply [his] imperfection."[30] At the same time, Conway rejected certain aspects of scholastic philosophical theology, arguing that "indifference of will" (which she associated with the scholastic conception of deity) was not a feature of God, but rather an imperfection found in humans. She believed that the quality of "indifference of acting or not acting" could not belong to God, for it implied immutability and corruption. If one were to associate such indifference to divine reality, then God would become like "those cruel tyrants in the world who do most things from their own pure will, relying on their power, so that they are unable to give any explanation for their actions other than their own pure will."[31] According to Conway, God certainly was not indifferent about whether to give being to creatures; rather, creation occurred as a result of an inner impulse of divine goodness and wisdom.

In her brief, albeit provocative, section on Christology, Conway described Christ as the crucial link between God and the rest of creation: "By the son of God (the first born of all creatures, whom we Christians call Jesus Christ, according to Scripture, as shown above), is understood not only his divinity but his humanity in eternal union with the Divinity; that is, his celestial humanity was united with the Divinity before the creation of the world and before his incarnation."[32] In this same section, Conway elaborated on Christ's unique status in the cosmological ordering, that is, that the Christ figure was of a "lesser nature" than God, yet "greater" than all remaining creatures. As an intermediary being, Christ made possible the continuum between God and the rest of creation. Through the Christ principle, God also communicated life, actions, goodness, and justice. In Conway's theological cosmology, the Christ figure was also the medium through which creation occurred.

Showing her indebtedness to kabbalistic literature, Conway explicitly referenced one of its central figures, Adam Kadmon.

> The ancient Kabbalists have written many things about this, namely, how the son of God was created; how his existence in the order of nature preceded all creatures; how everything is blessed and receives holiness in him and through him, whom they call in their writings the celestial Adam, or the first man Adam Kadmon, the great priest, the husband or betrothed of the church, or as Philo Judaeus called him, the first-born son of God.[33]

In the Lurianic Kabbalah, Adam Kadmon is the Primordial Man linking God, humanity, and the world—a rich metaphor suggesting that the cosmos is very much akin to a living human organism, and that the world, as created by God, itself has interests and values that resonate with those of humanity. Conway's identification of Christ with Adam Kadmon contained important and fascinating theological implications, which, unfortunately, she did not fully develop in the text. Moreover, Conway did not provide a fuller exposition of how her view differed from established Trinitarian doctrine, so one can only conjecture as to the extent of her radical departure from orthodox Christian teachings of the period.

Unlike the Christ figure, which only changed for the better, other created nature in Conway's system moved toward either goodness or badness. As noted earlier, created substance, like God, consisted of spirit; unlike God, however, it was constitutive of particles called monads. All creation also was alive, and capable of perception and motion. When distinguishing divine nature from the rest of creation, Conway thus pointed to creaturely nature as mutable, capable of changing from one state to another. She then differentiated between two kinds of change: (1) the intrinsic power to change either for good or bad (common to all creatures), and (2) the ability to move only from one good to another good (found only in the Christ figure).

The pervasive sentience that Conway detected in the created order was firmly rooted in her conception of divine nature, which generated a participatory goodness permeating all of creation. Although created nature did not share in God's incommunicable traits (e.g., aseity, independence, immutability, infinity, and perfection), it did share other communicable ones. Conway asserted, "God is infinitely good and communicates [his] goodness to all [his] creatures in infinite ways, so that there is no creature which does not receive something of [his] goodness. . . . Did not God create all [his] creatures to this end, namely, that they be blessed in [him] and enjoy [his] divine goodness in their various conditions and states? Moreover, how could this be possible without life or perception? How can anything lacking life enjoy divine goodness?"[34] Conway's celebration of creation's intrinsic power to move toward goodness provided potential transformative meaning for her contemporaries. She envisioned a natural order in which the fundamental, common feature of all creatures is the urge toward the fullness of life, or toward ultimate (divine) fulfillment.[35] In Conway's cosmological construction, where all natural processes constantly strive toward divinizing themselves, one also sees a variant of the alchemical axiom associated with transmutation: Everything in nature strives for perfection.

The perfectionism endemic to Conway's system could be understood in two senses. First, it implied an ontological (metaphysical) basis whereby all created things had the capacity of becoming more spirit-like, that is, more refined "spiritual" substance. Simultaneously, created natures were capable of increased goodness. With such a worldview, Conway departed from many of her orthodox Christian peers, appropriating some of the older mystical or occult forms of knowledge that she and van Helmont were studying. She seemed interested in developing the esoteric or spiritual side of alchemy, which, in turn, had built upon Gnostic and Neoplatonist ideas that had been expunged from orthodox Christianity. With her emphasis on nature's movement toward goodness and on its processional ontology, Conway also anticipated a fundamental aspect of twentieth-century process naturalism, namely, to be a sentient entity is to be in process. Indeed, for Conway, (human and nonhuman) creation's constitutive nature was to change and constantly evolve. This principle of immanent change permeating creation was a vital component of Conway's mystical naturalism, and it is precisely at this point that one can now make fuller sense of her particular reading of, and response to, Cartesian mechanism.

CONWAY'S REJECTION OF DESCARTES' DUALISM

According to Conway, Descartes may very well have described the world in sufficient terms, but he had not fully understood it. While agreeing with Descartes that the cosmos was composed of substances that have both thought and extension, Conway adamantly denied any ontological separateness of these two dimensions of reality, arguing instead for a monistic unity of spirit and matter. She believed that by denying the union of spirit and body, both ancient and modern philosophies "have generally erred and laid a poor foundation in the very beginning, and thus their entire house and building is so weak and, indeed, so useless that the whole edifice must collapse in time."[36] Conway rejected any notion of dualism because of its logical separation of matter and spirit, of nonconscious and conscious qualities, and of world and God.

Directly challenging Descartes' dualism, Conway constructed the universe as a vitalistic, organic unity. She argued that all existents (from God through Christ to nondivine creation) were one substance, which "varie[d] according to its modes of existence, one of which [wa]s corporeality."[37] Created beings or species were modes of this one single substance that was comprised of an infinite number of hierarchally arranged particles or monads. These monads were either spiritual or material, and both matter and spirit were composed of parts that have extension. Those parts that made up the spiritual were lighter, ethereal elements; those that constituted the material were heavier, darker elements. In such a system, that which was commonly taken to be matter was in fact less refined spirit—congealed spirit, as it were. The spiritual combined with the material through a middle element, an element lighter than matter and heavier than spirit. Furthermore, Conway argued, body and spirit were not contrary entities, the first impenetrable and divisible, the latter penetrable and indivisible, as More and other Platonists assumed. Rather, both spirit and matter were locatable in time and space, were divisible, and influenced each other. Between all created contingent beings there was a continuum of mind and body, some substances tending more toward the mental than the physical, and vice versa—but never to the extent of reaching God's essence, which, for Conway, was ethereal.[38]

In a fashion akin to other organic thinkers of her era, Conway based her system of creation on a great hierarchical chain of being, modified to incorporate an evolution or transmutation to higher forms, and based on the acquisition of goodness and perfection. In her worldview, every substance was capable of being changed from thought to matter as well as from matter to thought. Monads appearing more like matter implied a falling away from the goodness of God. By the same token, the purification of substances to become more spirit-like involved a return toward goodness—toward God. In addition, creatures could move up or down the ontological scale, transmuting into higher or lower orders of creatures. For example, through a succession of transmutations, natural objects such as sand or dust could acquire the noblest attributes of substance, that is, "a capacity for all kind of feeling, perception, or knowledge, even love, all power and virtue, joy and fruition."[39] Conway's cosmological system also contained certain perspectives that seem incredible to us today: stone and dust could eventually be transformed (logically) into human beings. The reverse was also true. An individual could become a stone or a horse could become a shrub. Beyond the fact that there was no essential difference between spirit and body, the two were inconvertible and an intimate, organic bond and unity existed between them.[40]

The concept of transmigration that Conway described is a crucial one also found in Isaac Luria's cosmology, suggesting strong kabbalistic influences on her cosmological perspectives. For instance, Luria employed the idea of animal metempsychosis in elaborate schemata in influential writings, arguing that a human may become an animal or even a vegetable if its behavior in a previous life has been brutish or vegetal. He wrote, "There are few men who are able to avoid revolution in some animal or vegetable, and similarly in some other creature of the world. For which reason everyone is compelled to undergo his punishment in both body and soul because he is brought into a certain bodily state in order that he might be able to feel those pains which he merits. And all things happened according to the nature of the sin."[41]

CONWAY'S MYSTICISM NATURALISM
AND THE LURIANIC KABBALAH

As I discussed in chapter 2, Conway preferred the more positive Lurianic teachings on human nature to the pessimistic ones found in the influential Calvinistic theological tradition. She also incorporated variants of Luria's mythical cosmology into her text, and several of his basic doctrines provide a conceptual basis for understanding some of Conway's crucial views regarding nature's progress toward divine goodness and concerning human nature's movement in an aesthetic, ethical monistic cosmos. His theories also helped shape Conway's intriguing moral interpretation of human pain (or a type of theodicy). In Luria's fuller explanation of creation and the ultimate redemption of things, theogony (self-manifestation of divinity) and cosmogony (manifestation of the cosmos) are inextricably intertwined. His complex system conceived the first act of God (*Ein-Sof*) as withdrawal or *tsimtsum* (literally, contraction or shrinkage), leaving a void within which finite things can subsist: "When [*Ein-Sof*] determined to create its world and to issue forth the world of emanated entities, to bring to light the fullness of His energies [literally, "activities"], names, and qualities, this being the reason for the creation of the world. . . . *Ein-Sof* then withdrew itself from its centermost point, at the center of its light, and this light retreated from the center to the sides, and thus remained a free space, an empty vacuum."[42] In the Lurianic myth, this void becomes the metaphysical space in which *Ein-Sof* emanates an infinity of worlds and beings, the first of which is Adam Kadmon, who is also the precursor of all things, the first being who emerges after the *tsimtsum* and the vehicle through which the *sefirot* (vessels) and the worlds are emanated. Luria believed the *sefirot* were emanated as lights from the ear, nose, mouth, and eyes of Adam Kadmon. These lights both emanate and return, leaving behind a residue from which the vessel for each *sefirah* is formed.

In his mythos, Luria elaborated on two earlier kabbalistic doctrines: the "breaking of the vessels" (*shevirath-ha-kelim*) and restoration (*tikkun*)—both showing that evil and sin are the temporary products of disorder. There are different versions of what happens next in the myth, based on which disciple or student's interpretation one reads. According to one version, further divine lights burst forth from Adam Kadmon, but the vessels meant to contain them shattered. With the "breaking of the vessels," evil comes into the world and souls are sunk in matter—or, as Luria explained it in a more poetic sense: "the shattered pieces of the broken vessels fell down and became the dregs of the material world, while the purest and most divine parts of the lights of the *sefirot* (which these vessels were meant to contain) fell back to the heavens. Some sparks of light, however, fell with the vessels and became immersed in matter; these were the souls in exile."[43] In Lurianic thought, exile was both a requisite to creation and the cause of evil and sin. Consequently, the work of restoration (*tikkun*) involved freeing these sparks, or souls, from their exiled state, trapped in material prisons, and reuniting them with the divine light.

For Luria, it was only through human actions that the souls, trapped among the shards of broken vessels, could be reunited with the divine light. His historiography revealed a constant struggle between the forces of good and evil, in which subsequent generations from Adam up to the present participate in the process of *tikkun*. This mythic struggle between good and evil was played out over and over until Kabbalists, who experienced repeated reincarnations (*gilgun*), became perfect. Luria thus introduced a practical mysticism involving activist, historical forces, through which Kabbalists engaged in a cosmic drama of universal salvation. For him, Kabbalists were not supposed to retreat into their own private world and bemoan the loss of an ideal past. Rather, their task was to repair that loss and restore the world to pristine perfection. With its optimistic philosophy of perfectionism and universal salvation, Luria's universe was restored to its original perfection through human effort.[44] Although the process of *tikkun* may be long and arduous, restoration will eventually occur as each exiled being moved up the ladder of creation, becoming morally better and increasingly spiritual until finally freed from the cycle of rebirth.

A similar impetus toward perfection was also present in Conway's cosmology. Her readings in the *Kabbala denudata* helped solidify her belief in progress and her commitment to religious toleration, affirming her conviction that nature's progress toward goodness is inevitable and undeniable. For example, in Conway's depiction of nature's movement toward God, she evoked the process of *tikkun* when speaking of creatures' nature, which is to become more and more divinized, that is, more and more spiritually oriented—to infinity. For Conway, created nature's primary task was regenerating a state of goodness in which it had been created and from which it had fallen. Notably, creation could never fall again because it had acquired a greater perfection and strength in this life, and there seemed to be a regenerative principle at work in nature: "Hence one can infer that all God's creatures, which have previously fallen and degenerated from their original goodness, must be changed and restored after a certain time to a condition which is not simply as that in which they were created, but better."[45]

Conway's development of the monistic worldview found in *The Principles* also expressed aspects of Luria's cosmological system. An important assumption attached to the Lurianic Kabbalah was its ability to unlock the secrets of the two great books God had given humanity: the book of scripture and the book of nature. Both books—the first dealing with the upper world and the latter with the lower—were intimately linked. Accepting this truth claim, Conway proclaimed and justified another insight about observable reality, namely, that the perceived gap between the material and spiritual realms, or matter and spirit, was nonexistent. In her system, matter and spirit were simply different ends of a single continuum. As well, the distinction between body and spirit is only modal and incremental—not essential and substantial—indicating the very order of things. Conway described different expressions of love to exemplify the common nature that all creatures shared, even despite the different modalities that often appeared to humans. She believed that the basis of all love or desire, which attracted one thing to another, was the one nature and substance they all shared. Sounding like as an early modern naturalist, Conway advanced her theory while observing the behaviors of all species: "We also see that animals of the same species love each other more than animals of a different species. Thus cattle of one species graze together, birds of one species fly in flocks, fish of one species swim together, and [men] prefer to associate with [men] rather than with other creatures."[46] Beyond these particular forms of love, or natural affinity of one animal toward another, there was a universal love evident in all creatures because they all shared the same primary substance.

Conway considered Descartes' idea of an irreducible essential difference between body and spirit erroneous because he did not account for the interaction and vital agreement between body and spirit (or soul). Thus, in the midst of her complex theories concerning the unity of body and spirit, Conway also brought up an interesting point concerning pain. She suggested that the soul felt pain and grief when the body was cut or wounded, and that it suffered with and through the body, hence, the two must be united and of one substance.[47] For the sake of argument, Conway believed that a dualist may answer that only the body felt pain, not the soul. Yet, she said, such a response was inconsistent with the dualist's primary premise, that is, that the body itself did not have life or feeling in it. Princess Elizabeth, a mutual friend, also questioned Descartes about such matters in correspondence, sharing Conway's concern for the possible connections between the Cartesian (thinking) mind and the (nonthinking) body, and for the larger set of issues concerning the experiences of emotion and pain.[48] Sadly, Elizabeth's queries were dismissed by Descartes and remain curiously absent in later correspondence, and Conway's observations were not fully developed in her text. Yet, both women helped set the direction, however faintly, for later critiques of dualistic theories, in which mind and body, or reason and emotion, were antithetical. As many contemporary feminists contend, the characteristic logical structure of this philosophical dualism has resulted in various alienated forms of differentiation, pernicious denials of dependency, and problematic representations of otherness.

DEAD MATTER? CONWAY RESPONDS TO DESCARTES

As with the issue of dualism, Conway's general response to Descartes' view of dead matter was cast in theological terms. In her system, dead matter did not share in divine goodness in the least; nor was it capable of reason and able to acquire greater goodness to infinity, which was the nature of all creatures that grew and progressed infinitely toward greater perfection. She observed, "Since dead matter does not share any of the communicable attributes of God, one must then conclude that dead matter is completely non-being, a vain fiction and Chimera, and an impossible thing."[49] Using the vocabulary of the mechanics, Conway provided fuller reasoning for her views. While acknowledging that Descartes taught many "remarkable and ingenious things concerning the mechanical aspects of natural processes and about how all motions proceed according to regular mechanical laws," Conway still argued that the laws of local motion did not explain the vital operations of nature.[50] According to her reasoning, materialist explanations may have explained everything in terms of local and mechanical motion, but such reductionism failed to take account of the movements of life itself. In affirming this idea, Conway opposed Descartes and other mechanical philosophers who defined matter solely as extended body in motion and nothing more. She asserted, "They do not go beyond the husk and shell, nor ever reach the kernel. They only touch the surface, never glimpsing the center. For they ignore the most noble attribute of that substance, which they call matter and body, and understand nothing about it."[51] In short, for Conway, Descartes and the other mechanists failed to understand the limitations of their reductionistic physics.

As she developed her vitalistic model, Conway generally accepted an instrumental role for local motion in the operations of nature. Accordingly, local or mechanical motion allowed the body to be transported from one place to another. However, "vital action [wa]s a far more noble and divine way of operating than local motion."[52] For Conway, the changes that one might observe in a natural object's outward appearances were not the mere result of immediate and local change described by the mechanists; they were also the results of an organism's inner movement toward goodness. Vital action revealed the "wisdom, goodness, and power" intrinsically present in creatures that continue to perfect themselves as they participate in goodness.[53] While clearly different from local or mechanical motion, vital action was not separate from it. In addition, the particular configuration of any one body was only one attribute of its fundamental substance. With other vitalists, Conway evoked a particular important aspect of Aristotelian vitalism that had been superseded by the mechanists. Influenced by Aristotle, these thinkers viewed the soul as the form of the body—making it that particular body—and as the source of the vital functions of the body, rational, sensitive, and vegetative functions.[54]

As Conway saw it, mechanists described all vital functions of the body through the laws of physics, the ultimate explanation of the material world. Accordingly, Descartes' great error was imputing to creaturely activity only mechanical motion, forfeiting the value and import of vital motion—that of the living body. Conway thus distinguished between two features found in all creatures: material and virtual extension. The former was that which matter, body, or substance had, considered without motion or action. Regarding the latter, she wrote, "Virtual extension is the motion or action which a creature has whether given immediately from God or received from some fellow creature . . . every motion which proceeds from the proper life and will of a creature is vital, and I call this the motion of life, which clearly is neither local nor mechanical like the other kind but has in itself life and vital power."[55]

Conway believed interaction between creatures is by a process analogous to emanation or radiation. For example, the virtual extension, or a motion or action that a creature has, proceeded from its innermost parts and reached to other creatures through a proper spiritual medium. This spiritual principle of causality may be likened to a field of force, and provided the dynamics of perceptionism in Conway's ontology. The mechanistic idea that matter was merely the passive carrier of external forces was a useful concept to explain the way bodies interacted, but, for Conway, it was woefully insufficient—this conception would also be too simplistic to be used in later explanations of chemical reactions or biological processes.

The Principles is arguably one of the most provocative theological and philosophical texts written by a woman in the seventeenth century. In it, Conway attacked dualists for conceiving of matter as dead, for seeing mechanical motion as the only type of motion for material entities, and for failing to account for the interaction and communication between body and spirit. She also critiqued Descartes and other dualists for being inconsistent in formulating separate definitions of matter and spirit. In her countertradition, Conway argued that all of the created order (excluding the Christ figure) contained both material and spiritual units. This compositional unity accounted for the activity and sensibility of the body and the interactions between body and soul. As previously indicated, matter and spirit, for Conway, were not irreducible entities, so they shared the basic character of having extension, penetrability, and divisibility. While our contemporary knowledge may empirically validate such qualities in matter, it is not so obvious that the same empirical understanding can apply to Conway's particle theory of spirit. What, if anything, can one say of the nature of spiritual particles? Yet, despite these conceptual limitations,

Conway's thought remains historically significant for contemporary readers interested in probing further into the fullness of such notions as the real, the good, and the natural.

Out of the eclectic admixture of religious, mystical, and scientific beliefs characterizing Conway's system, a hermeneutic of nature gradually emerges, asserting that all of nature is essentially good and valuable. This basic maxim foreshadows contemporary liberationist perspectives that promote the intrinsic value of all forms of nature (particularly modern constructions of "human" nature). It is also reflected in the current ecological impetus that refuses to severe value from any connection with the natural (nonhuman) world. Yet, as certain developments in the West have shown, Conway's basic conceptual views and moral convictions regarding nature were overshadowed by influential scientific ideologies, which logically extended the conceptual dualism of seventeenth-century mechanism to later problematic gender and racial classifications. Whereas Descartes' conceptual dualism and mechanism were valorized, Conway's provocative vitalistic orientations were neglected and undermined within the received tradition of intellectual history. Later modern forms of analytical reason engineered an extraordinary transformation in our landscape and values, while the import of its thematic counterpart, vitalism, often faded in obscurity, recessing into controversy and muted silence, often lost to the charges of magic and sorcery. Although it is impossible to recover or even retain all of Conway's fascinating theory of nature today, I contend that reverberations and traces of her vitalistic discourse are still being felt and recovered in various spheres of humanistic thought today, and I discuss these fluctuating vibrational chords in the second part of this book.

PART 2

CHAPTER 4

Conway's Religious Vitalism, Visionary Countertraditions, and the "More" of Life

> Where is the life we have lost in living? Where is the wisdom we have lost in the knowledge? Where is the knowledge we have lost in information?
>
> —T. S. Eliot, *Choruses from the Rock*

Contemporary readers have the benefit of examining the richness and novelty of Conway's vitalistic ideas within seventeenth-century English religious thought and life, and of ascertaining her contribution to a trajectory of vitalistic discourse in the West. As I discussed in the first part of this study, Conway's exploration of esoteric and ancient wisdoms, and her creative exchanges with van Helmont and others, led her to conceptualize nature as a complex network of changing processes, where interior motives or purposive intent are endemic to all natural processes—a view of nature as alive and vibrant, evolving toward divine goodness. In addition, Conway was inspired by the Quakers' particular brand of mystical religiosity and by their radical enactments of love in the world to espouse an aesthetic-ethical cosmology that had major repercussions for understanding human relationality and self-actualization. Conway's convictions regarding natural processes arose, in part, from her adaptation of key doctrines found in the *Kabbala denudata*. Along with other esoteric depositories such as hermeticism, Renaissance Neoplatonism, and alchemy, Lurianic kabbalism saw humanity perfecting itself and the world.

This early modern emphasis on human actualization and self-transcendence—subtly and ingeniously expressed in Conway's religious naturalism—helped shape Enlightenment humanism, whose agenda became synonymous with such lofty, ennobling terms as equality, individual actualization, and progress. Yet, while Conway framed her distinct notions of human aspiration within a mystical, monistic cosmology that emphasized relationality among all entities, most Enlightenment thinkers abandoned her sacred vision of existence, establishing very different views of progress and individuality.[1] Seduced by the Cartesian turn to subjectivity and lured by the desire for an Archimedean point or foundation, they extended the logic of mechanism to affirm a new view of human progress, in which society legitimates its values and its representational knowledge via reason and science. Subsequently, post-Cartesian modernism developed into an episteme of representation, establishing the autonomous bourgeois and reducing the corporeal, relational, moral self to a pure object of knowledge, to consciousness of mind.

In this second part, I show that Conway's religious naturalism is part of a different legacy of modernism, and serves as a heuristic model for further religious and philosophical reflections on natural processes. I consider of particular value Conway's ingenuity in exposing the error of viewing mechanism as the sole explanatory model for nature, which reduced active, purposive life to its functionary level and aided in the creation of an impoverished, desacralized world. When nature has been conceived as lacking vital intentionality, non-human forms of it have been instrumentalized, ultimately set apart from humans, and put to use as humans see fit. In contrast, Conway's early modern discourse advanced rich conceptualizations of nature that helped convey the uniqueness (or the "more") of life.

I believe that Conway's unique set of discursive formations encourages contemporary religionists to embark on the quintessentially postmodern religious task of challenging reductionism in any form, or of resisting what Theodore Roszak identifies as "that peculiar sensibility which degrades what it studies by depriving its subject of charm, autonomy, dignity, mystery."[2] I also think that Conway's ideas are pivotal in foregrounding a crucial set of Euro-American debates in subsequent centuries between vitalists and mechanists regarding the "nature" of nature. Some of these lively discussions and developments contributed to the emergence of twentieth-century process metaphysics, which I consider one of the most viable strains of religious naturalism today. In conjoining specific theories of vitalism with process thought, I trace a trajectory of religious naturalism, another modernism, that Conway had a pivotal role in advancing. I emphasize, of course, that Conway could not be mistaken for a process theologian—her theism retained too many elements of scholastic rationalism and harbored residual Platonism. She, however, certainly pushed us in the right direction in the seventeenth century in formulating a conception of creation (indeed, a cosmology) where the vital operations of nature convey much more than the mechanists allowed—indeed, she conceived a world in which an increase of goodness, beauty, and love as transformative occurs as processional nature actualizes itself.[3]

VITALISM AND MECHANISM IN HISTORICAL PERSPECTIVE

Vitalism is a concept that has been at the center of significant developments in Western intellectual life, even though it ceases to be an influential one in current debates. As a general category of analysis, vitalism is primarily associated with a distinct set of perspectives and developments pertaining to the constitutive nature of life or organisms. Sometimes as philosophers, artists, and religionists, other times as scientists, vitalists in the West have advocated the active presence of some principle or force in addition to the physical components of the living organism. In its most sustained form, emerging from eighteenth-century scientific and philosophical developments, modern vitalism declared that the activity of organisms could not be totally (or solely) explained by mechanistic theory, which affirmed that such activity is innate to matter, ordered according to its material structure. Opposing such zealous reductionism, vitalists introduced some extra material or element to material structure.

One of the earliest intimations of vitalism (or, perhaps a proto-vitalist position) can be found in Aristotle (384–322 B.C.E.), who, along with other theorists, raised the question of whether (and how) life is related to the material substance in which it manifests itself. In his natural philosophy, Aristotle distinguished between matter and form, yet, at the same time, linked the two through a distinct process of development. Matter, for Aristotle, contained the essential nature of all things, but only as a potential—the essence becomes real, or actual, via form.[4] In other words, Aristotle posited matter as potency for form, where a thing's form was its essential or defining characteristics. The form of any inorganic or organic thing was its act, so that, for Aristotle, form was not inserted in some already existing body, but constituted the body to be what it was from within itself.

The natural world, as Aristotle conceived it, exhibited a collective dynamic that affected the transition from mere possibilities for a sector of nature to the realization of its full potential, its perfection (*entelecheia*).[5] Accordingly, biological form was more than shape, more than a static configuration of components in a whole—there was a continual flux of matter through a living organism, while its form was maintained. Aristotle considered form the highest expression of being, and argued that matter was never found without form. He identified the process of self-actualization of the essence in the actual phenomenon as *entelechy* ("self-completion"), where matter and form were the two sides of the process, separable only through abstraction.[6] Although Aristotle's metaphysics was a type of substantialism, it was nonetheless pervasively processional and teleological. Additionally, while Aristotelian physics has for the most part been discarded in the evolution of Western thought, his notion of some apparent purpose of ordered growth and development of organic form has posed a challenge to even the most committed mechanists.

Vitalistic concepts and imagery were also advanced in the work of another ancient Greek thinker, Galen, the physician (131–201 C.E.), who constructed fascinating theories in ancient biology. In his explorative studies in anatomy and physiology, Galen rejected the notion that exquisitely designed organisms could be explained solely in terms of the mindless interaction of atoms. Galen thought that blood, which reaches the left side of the heart from the lungs and then surges through the arteries as rich red arterial blood, was charged with a vital principle or vital spirit. This fundamental principle of life, in Galenic physiology, was pneuma (air, breath), which took three forms in the liver, heart, and brain, controlling such things as the passions, senses, and consciousness.[7]

Galen's theories adapted very well to later Christian doctrines and his work became the standard epistemological model for medical studies in subsequent centuries, expressed most vividly in the work of physicians during the medieval period. Establishing anatomy as the foundation of medical knowledge, Galen frequently dissected and experimented on such animals as African monkeys, pigs, sheep, and goats, which resulted in his anatomical work on humans containing various inaccuracies. Even when Western Europeans began to practice human dissection in the later Middle Ages, instruction in anatomy still relied on Galen's model. For example, while a professor read a text of Galen on anatomy, an assistant dissected a cadaver for illustrative purposes.[8]

Medieval physiology also reflected Galenic hypotheses, including the belief that there were two separate blood systems: one controlling muscular activities and containing bright red blood moving upward and downward through the arteries; the other governing the digestive functions and containing dark red blood that ebbed and flowed in the veins. Due to Galen's enduring legacy, vitalistic imagery remained prominent in early medical philosophies throughout the sixteenth and seventeenth centuries. Many traditional healing practices considered disease to be the result of some imbalance in the vital energies that distinguished living from nonliving matter; physicians often identified these vital forces as the humours.[9]

In the mid-seventeenth century, Conway's refutation of Descartes' *diesseigkeit* was a crucial moment in this vitalistic trajectory. On the one hand, it exemplified the inevitable consequence of the Aristotelian legacy that differentiated between substance (structure, matter, quantity) and form (pattern, order, quality). On the other hand, Conway's resistance to the reductionism of Cartesian mechanical philosophy helped to set the stage for an ongoing polemic between mechanism and holism—a theme that would be repeatedly reiterated in subsequent centuries between those supporting some form of vitalism and those having a profound faith in mechanical reductionism. Descartes and his successors extended mechanistic explanations of natural phenomena to biological systems, maintaining that animals, and the human body, were 'automata,' or mechanical devices, differing from artificial devices only in terms of their degree of complexity. Despite the efforts of Conway and other vitalists, the metaphor of the machine that Descartes and other mechanists inaugurated became an influential and fruitful notion for later thinkers, many of whom began drawing attention to the role of the various organs of the human anatomy, as opposed to vital forces, in the maintenance of life. Furthermore, with the invention of the microscope in the seventeenth century, as well as sophisticated developments of germ theory of disease in Western medicine, the potent and direct challenges to vitalistic theories increased.[10]

Descartes' model of analytical thinking, which consisted in breaking up complex phenomena into pieces to understand the behavior of the whole from the properties of the parts, was also influential in later empirical developments in the sciences. Cartesian mechanism was often expressed in the growing assumption among scientists that the laws of biology were ultimately reducible to those of physics and chemistry. In his polemic treatise, *Man a Machine* (1748), Julien de La Mettrie offered an elaborate and persuasive expression of totalizing mechanistic physiology, which remained popular well beyond the eighteenth century and generated many debates and controversies—some reaching as far as the twentieth century.[11] Although simplistic mechanical models of living organisms were largely abandoned in the early nineteenth century, the essence of Cartesian mechanism survived in some shape. Some thinkers, for instance, still viewed animals as machines (albeit much more complicated than mechanical clockworks) involving complex chemical processes.

The new discoveries in astronomy, physics, and mathematics, associated with the names of Copernicus, Galileo, Descartes, and Bacon, eventually led to a paradigm shift in which the world became a perfect machine governed by exact mathematical laws, whose parts moved and interacted according to discernible patterns of cause and effect, rather than according to unpredictable internal impulses. This vision of a mechanized world reached its fullest completion in Isaac Newton, whose grand synthesis of mechanics became the hallmark of seventeenth-century science. A metaphysical position of radical reductionism informed the Newtonian universe, where everything was reduced to a set of basic elements (e.g., particles or atoms) that were external to one another and had no interiority themselves. Furthermore, each particle was independent of the nature of other particles, and since the elements or particles only interacted mechanically, the forces of interaction did not affect inner natures. The Newtonian worldview celebrated an ontology of substance, in which material things and everything were part of a machine, comprising independent parts, each adapted for a specific function and moving in a specific manner within the machine.[12] Its epistemological assertion was clear: once the initial conditions and the force laws were given, everything was calculable forever, before and after. The world, viewed as a system, was governed completely by the laws of mechanics and of conservation of energy. In a fundamental sense, it was totally determined.

The Newtonian worldview also generated important theological questions concerning divine activity in nature and in the cosmos. What was the role of God in a universe that ran like a clock? Was divine action restricted to the initial creation of a law-bound system and thereby opposed to the Christian conception of subsequent revelation in the universe? How effective was divine providence, or God's watchful concern for the lives of the individuals, in a cosmos where all events were ultimately reducible to mechanical laws? At this juncture, even though many scientists reexamined the notion of divine purpose within the context of discovering physical laws governing celestial and terrestrial mechanics, they did not immediately abandon it. For example, Newton saw in such eternal, immutable laws of motion an expression of the splendor and majesty of a rational deity. According to Newton, the universe may be a giant mechanism, like a clock, but a wonderful clock nonetheless. Although ordered and predictable, the universe's workings were upheld by a perpetual miracle.[13] Unfortunately, in the prevalent accounts of Western science, these theological aspects of Newton's thought were submerged and marginalized, even privatized, while his mechanical reductionism was publicized and celebrated.

COUNTERTRADITIONS AND WHOLISTIC VISIONS CELEBRATING NATURE'S "MORE"

The binary structure driving Newton's approach to nature (e.g., its public/mechanical and private/religious features) can be viewed as a wonderful example of the complexities, ambiguities, and paradoxes associated with the Cartesian-Baconian-Newtonian discursive model. With impassioned intensity, this modernist trajectory ordered and classified natural processes, ultimately reducing them to the categories of mechanism. However, as various natural philosophers, religious humanists, and mystical poets have proposed, and a few holistic scientists have tried to demonstrate, the full, transparent knowledge of natural life desired by this dominant strain has yet to be—perhaps can never be—achieved, as the myriad, processional forms of nature constantly illustrate the futilities, fissures, and excesses of such epistemological tyranny. As Conway's reflections in the seventeenth century suggest, the nonreducible, stubbornly otherness of nature has often found expression in religious inquiry, or in aesthetical, ethical mystical visions of nature, which have inspired humans to engage in benevolent, meaningful acts of world-formation. Later, in the eighteenth and nineteenth centuries, various Romantic artists, philosophers, and poets also envisioned the "more" of nature, signaling the presence of imaginative (albeit subjugated) epistemologies that refuse to be eradicated.

Echoing some of Conway's early modern concerns, William Blake (1757–1827), a key figure among the English Romantics, conceived of nature as an organic whole. Using the macro-micro analogy, Blake and other visionaries also considered humans to be more than a collection of separate atoms. Embodying the Romantic vision, Blake targeted the reductionism of Newton that ensued from the mechanistic Cartesian paradigm. To his friend Thomas Butts, he passionately wrote:

> May God us keep
> From single vision & Newtons sleep.[14]

As Conway resisted the myopic vision of Descartes, so Blake refuted Newton's single vision, which disintegrated the natural landscape, reducing it to bits and pieces. Blake and other Romantics believed nature should not be divorced from aesthetic values, which, for them, were just as real (or even more real) than the abstractions of science. Although mechanism was certainly helpful in discovering how the world works, to the Romantic vision of life, it could not fully convey worlds of meaning and love, or successfully illustrate humanity's playful and responsible engagement with otherness.

Sharing some of Blake's concerns, various German Romantic poets and philosophers revived the Aristotelian tradition and concentrated on the nature of organic form as they faced a modern crisis of consciousness produced by reductionistic epistemologies. Johann Wolfgang von Goethe (1749–1832), a central figure in this movement, constructed a natural philosophy aimed at rescuing the study of nature from militant scientific reductionism. In his scientific philosophy, Goethe used the term "morphology" to describe biological form from a dynamic, developmental point of view.[15] Admiring nature's moving order (*bewegliche Ordnung*), Goethe conceived of form as a pattern of relationships within an organized whole—a conception that is now in vogue in contemporary systems thinking. Goethe believed that each creature was a patterned gradation (*Schattierung*) of one great harmonious whole.[16] German Romantic artists were concerned primarily with a qualitative understanding of patterns, placing much emphasis on explaining the basic properties of life in terms of visualized forms. Goethe, too, felt that visual perception was an important avenue to understanding organic form. He believed nature held a pervasive pattern of process, of formation and transformation, which was accessible to the human observer by way of a certain type of introspection and observation—what Theodore Roszak later identifies as "contemplative non-intervention."[17]

Robert Richards notes that in Goethe's readings of Immanuel Kant's *Critique of Pure Judgment*, Goethe found a helpful demonstration of the intimate connections between biological science and art.[18] Although Kant believed that science offered only mechanical explanations, he also conceded that certain arenas (organic phenomena—especially reproduction) yielded such explanations inadequate—here scientific knowledge needed to be supplemented by visions of nature as purposeful. Consequently, as Richards suggests, for Kant, the limited scope of the mechanistic principle led to the assumption that biology could not really be a science, but at best only a loose system of uncertain empirical regularities, not a *Naturwissenschaft*, but a *Naturlehre*.[19] This conclusion notwithstanding, Kant's approach to the nature of living organisms contained a very important insight, that is, that organisms, in contrast with machines, were self-producing, self-organizing wholes. For example, in a machine, the parts only existed for each other, in the sense of supporting each other within a functional whole. In an organism, however, Kant asserted, the parts also existed *by means of* each other, in the sense of producing one another. He advised us to "think of each part as an organ that produces the other parts (so that each reciprocally produces the other) . . . Because of this, [the organism] will be both an organized and self-organizing being."[20]

Kant's suggestive idea regarding some type of interiority to nature (the notion of self-organization) inspired Goethe to advance a philosophic view of nature that reverberated with some of Conway's own insights regarding processional nature as a myriad complex of processes constituted by relationality, interior subjectivity, and intentionality. In his scientific works, Goethe spoke of a "formative impulse," which he believed to be operative in every organism. This driving force caused an organism to form itself according to its own distinct laws, such that rational laws or fiats could not be imposed at all from a higher, transcendent sphere.

Inspired by the life of nature, Goethe often articulated his observations of natural phenomena in very complex and beautiful poems. In *One and All* (1821), for instance, he described animated nature, evoking a world that engages humans, yet refuses to be entrapped by, or reduced to, humanity's limited comprehension and governance. In the poem, one hears faint mystical tonations, drawing human attention to the movements of vital life that mere mechanism can never fully describe or comprehend.

One and All

in boundlessness, itself discovering there,
the singular would gladly disappear.
satiety is then absolved quite;
ardent wishing, savage will abate,
strict obligation, coping, ah, with fate:
in self-abandon is delight.

soul of the world, soak into us, descend,
then with the very welgeist to contend

our finest faculties contract:
spirits beneign will guide and sympathize,
sublimest masters gently ways devise
to the perpetual creative act.

and with effect to make creation new,
its weaponed rigor soon enough undo,
action eternal, vivid, rose;
and what was not, now wishes to unfold,
become unsullied suns, a colored world:
no circumstance permits repose.

it has to move, to be creating deed,
first make its form, then, changing it, proceed;
all stopping, short-illusion's twist.
for the eternal onward moves in all,
and into nothing everything must fall,
if it in being would persist.[21]

Goethe conceived the fundamental nature of the world in aesthetic terms, simultaneously seeking a personal, intuitive, and individualized form of expression and polity of natural processes, and firmly supporting the Kantian idea of self-regulating and organic systems. His (Goethe's) vision of the subjectivity of nature is remarkable in its ability to capture the endless interplay within and among natural processes. Even more fascinating is the insight that humanity's own grasp of this truth yields fuller comprehension of its own dynamic participation in natural life. In *Parabasis*, another poem, Goethe observed that "all things to their type attest/self-insistent, always changing/near and far and far and near/birth of shapes/their rearranging—wonder of wonders, I am here."[22]

Goethe's natural philosophy contained a remarkable vision of nature that accentuated in subtle philosophical language the creative mystical tonations of Conway's early modern discourse—in both of their reflections, vital nature supercedes what we observe as necessarily functionary and adequately descriptive. Goethe's scientific observations, however, advanced far beyond Conway's speculative rationalism, and were quite distinct from her Christian idealism. He wrote:

One may conceive of the individual animal as a small world, existing for its own sake, by its own means. Every creature is its own reason to be. All its parts have a direct effect on one another, a relationship to one another, thereby constantly renewing the circle of life; thus we are justified in considering every animal physiologically perfect. Viewed from within, no part of the animal is a useless or arbitrary product of the formative impulse (as so often thought). Externally, some parts may seem useless because the inner coherence of the animal nature has given them this form without regard to outer circumstance. Thus . . . [not] the question, What are they for? but rather, Where do they come from?[23]

Goethe's aesthetic approach to nature was organic rather than geometrical, evolving rather than created, and based on sensibility and intuition, rather than on imposed order, culminating in a "living quality" in which the subject and object are dissolved together in a poise of inquiry. While Goethe embraced neither teleological nor deterministic views of growth within every organism, it is noteworthy that he rejected the mechanistic views that contemporaneous science subsumed during his time, denying rationality's superiority as the sole interpretation of reality.[24] And, even as he emphasized the functional value of knowledge, Goethe also advanced a view of it that presupposed much more. Knowledge, for him, had perspectival quality that expanded the truth of natural observation to a contextual grounding that was irreducible. He eloquently expressed such quality in the following poetic verses:

> Science of Nature has one goal:
> To find both manyness and Whole,
> Nothing "inside" or "Out there,"
> The "outer" world is all "In Here."
> Thus mysterious grasp without delay,
> This secret always on display.
> The true illusion celebrate,
> Be joyful in the serious game!
> No living thing lives separate:
> One and many are the same.[25]

VITALISTS AND MECHANISTS:
POLEMICS IN LATE MODERNISM

During the eighteenth and early nineteenth centuries, various thinkers wrestled with the fuller epistemological import of the mechanistic model, which often failed in practical, specific applications. Vitalists of various persuasions stated that living things could not be explained solely in terms of their physical and chemical constituents; rather, they argued, something in organisms—a nonmaterial element or a vital force—helped to differentiate them from inanimate things. In the field of medicine in the mid-eighteenth century, Montpellier physicians advanced a vitalist agenda in their attempts to contest the Cartesian dualist concept of the body-machine that was being championed by leading Parisian medical mechanists. Seeking to replace the body-machine dogma that sought laws universally valid for all phenomena, these vitalists posited a distinction between living and other matter, offering a holistic understanding of the physical-moral relation in place of mind-body dualism. Their medicine was not based on mathematics and the unity of the sciences, but on observation of the individual patient and the harmonious activities of the "body-economy." These French vitalists believed that illness was a result of disharmony in bodily processes that could only be remedied on an individual level depending on the patient's own 'natural' limitations. They established these limitations by a myriad of factors such as sex, class, age, temperament, region, and race, which negated the use of a single universal treatment for a particular ailment.[26]

The Romantic view of nature as "one great harmonious whole," in the Goethean sense, inspired some visionary scientists to extend their search for wholeness to the entire planet and to see the earth as an integrated whole, a living being. The lingering effects of the Romantic movement were evident in those scientists who endeavored to accept the implications of science without abandoning their religious faith, producing a brand of vitalism (sustained by several versions of the mind-body dualism) featuring spiritual animation amid the works of physical law. Developments such as Antoine Lavoisier's analysis of combustion, and his demonstration that respiration is a special form of oxidation, inspired some chemists in the early nineteenth century to confirm the relevance of chemical processes to the functioning of living organisms. They asserted that organic compounds were apparently formed only in living organisms, and thus appeared to be products of vital activity.

A good example of the relationship of chemistry to vitalist physiology was Justus Liebig's study of chemical reactions in plants and animals, which was published in 1842.[27] In his study of animals, Liebig was particularly interested in processes of metabolism and offered detailed chemical analyses of the sequence of reactions, based on chemical analysis of the foods taken in, the products absorbed, and the waste products released. Liebig conceived of some form of regulation for these reactions, thus positing a vital force that controlled them. According to Liebig, chemical and vital processes operated in opposite ways, and consequently both sorts of process were necessary in order to understand metabolism. In his study, Liebig evoked vital forces to explain phenomena that lacked ordinary explanation. These forces were comparable to other physical forces such as gravitational and chemical ones, but were also manifest under certain conditions. Accordingly, the vital forces possessed a peculiar property that was possessed by certain material bodies, becoming sensible when elementary particles were combined in a certain arrangement or form. Liebig concluded, "The vital force does not act, like the force of gravitation or the magnetic force, at infinite distances, but, like chemical forces, it is active only in the case of immediate contact. It becomes sensible by means of an aggregation of material particles."[28]

Despite these interesting examples from the fields of medicine and chemistry, scientific experiments in the nineteenth century steadily eroded support for vitalism in the West. Later chemical and anatomical discoveries pushed aside the "vital force" explanation, as numerous life processes were increasingly described in purely scientific terms, and as the medical model of disease drew more attention to the failure of particular organs and processes in the body. An example of this shift was the changing perspective of scientists toward organic compounds. Whereas the scientific community had once assumed organic compounds were produced by living organisms, as a by-product of the presence of vital forces, advances in chemical techniques eventually led scientists to assert that many of these compounds, such as urea, could be produced using the same types of chemical processes that produced inorganic compounds.[29] Furthermore, in the late nineteenth century, the mechanistic metaphor employed to construe the modern worldview was strengthened, in part, by three developments: the mechanistic account of evolution suggested by Darwin's principle of adaptation through natural selection; the discovery in physiology that the brain is a vast and complex of reflex nerve paths; and the formulation of the laws of thermodynamics.

Vitalistic theories resurged yet again in the late nineteenth and early twentieth centuries, primarily as a reaction against the reductionism of materialist scientists. At this juncture, however, developments in physics and chemistry had proceeded at a phenomenal pace, generating an extraordinary faith in the scientific method's ability to uncover all of life's secrets. In this context, the issue of vitalism became part of biological discourse and primarily concerned with assessing the uniqueness of life. And while the debate among theorists was still whether or not the phenomenon of the activity of life could be explained in purely mechanistic formulations, mechanism had evolved beyond that of Conway's era to refer to the position that all occurrences in the phenomenal world followed material laws.

At this juncture, mechanism was associated with an absolute principle of cosmic order, whose primary function was causal predetermination of all events. For scientists, many laws shared an attribute of absoluteness because they could be interpreted as consistent formulations of the single absolute law of cosmic order. Furthermore, with the discovery of the microscope in the latter part of the nineteenth century, together with advances in biology and the increasing successes in microbiology and embryology, scientists gave overwhelming credence to the view that life itself was, at heart, a mechanical process. Many of the strong reactions against mechanism during this period were due to the boldness with which physical science applied itself to the phenomenon of life. As Conway resisted the reductionistic mechanism of the seventeenth century to grasp the fullness of life, certain thinkers, mainly students of biology, again argued that life could not be explained solely in mechanistic terms.

A key figure in the early twentieth century was the German biologist and philosopher, Hans Driesch, a leading advocate of epigenesis. In his system of thought, Driesch saw evolution as producing more than the potential already present in matter. Elaborating on the premise that a living organism is more than a mere machine, Driesch recovered Aristotle's word *entelechy* to describe a vital force in developing his theory of epigenesis.[30] Following his pioneering work on the sea urchin, Driesch realized that after destroying one cell at the early two cell stage of a developing embryo, the remaining cell still developed into a complete sea urchin, not half an urchin—such an operation, he argued, could not be explained purely in mechanical terms. According to Driesch, no machine was able to go through such a series of divisions and remain what it was. Hence, biological reality seemed to indicate an ultimate plurality of life forms, which presented obstacles to mechanistic language with its reductionistic orientations and all-encompassing scope. Driesch spoke of a vital force, or a teleological factor, in the universe, which was simple in itself, yet appeared in diverse operations within the organism. This intensive manifoldness ordered each part to the whole, giving to the organism its reality as a living being. In the final analysis, for Driesch, this principle of life was "a factor in nature that acts teleologically."[31]

Driesch's desire to account for the fullness of life beyond mechanism was shared by the French philosopher Henri Bergson, another important representative of the countertradition that I trace here. In rejecting reductionism of any sort in the twentieth century while advancing vitalist imagery inclusive of scientific, philosophical, and religious concerns, Bergson embraced a spirit of inquiry that compelled Conway in the seventeenth century and inspired the Romantics in the eighteenth and nineteenth centuries. Bergson regarded process and temporality as crucial features of the natural world, and as central to our human scheme—for him, life and consciousness manifested change everywhere. In *Creative Evolution* (1907), Bergson argued that evolution, which he accepted as scientific fact, could not be reduced to mechanistic structure, but rather was driven by an *élan vital* (vital impulse or living energy).[32] In developing his philosophy of life, Bergson critiqued those philosophical interpretations of evolution theory that failed to see the importance of duration, which bore upon the very uniqueness of life. For him, the whole evolutionary process was best viewed as the endurance of an *élan vital* that was continually developing and generating new forms; in short, evolution was creative, not mechanistic.

Underlying Bergson's system of thought was the assumption of there being two very distinct ways of knowing: analytical and intuitive. The former understood reality in terms of stability, predictability, and spatial location; intuition, on the other hand, experienced growth, novelty, and temporal duration. According to Bergson, analytical knowledge was useful for getting things done, for acting on the world, yet it failed to reach the essential reality of things precisely because it left out duration and its perpetual flux, which is inexpressible and grasped only by intuition. In his processional philosophy, Bergson continued to explore the meaning and implications of his theory of intuition of duration as constituting the innermost reality of everything. His metaphysical system was one that rejected static values while embracing dynamic ones such as motion, change, and evolution.

For Bergson, nature was constituted by a *nisus* or striving to bring to realization something more, something over and above the existing frame of things. Change, innovation, and creativity were nature's essence and organic life in their most powerful expression. This mystical notion asserted that in addition to the complex organization of physical matter that went into making up living organisms, there must also be some nonmaterial, spiritual something-or-other added in that brought the entity to life. This inexhaustible, vital impulse oriented all of creation to greater perfection and as such lay at the core of evolution. According to Bergson, the original "life force" was passed down from one generation to another in all living things, and was the necessary creative force in an organism, which produced growth, guided development, and formed new adaptations. Accordingly, both evolution and *élan vital*—organic life's driving force of creativity and innovation—were everywhere at work. Within the human sphere, we experience them in our own activities, and, above all, in our own acts of free will.[33] According to the logic of this system, true duration was experienced only in the human person, and that duration was preserved in memory. While being informed by sense impressions, memory was not absolutely dependent on the matter of the brain. Finally, freedom was the personal event of self-creation.

In a later work, *The Two Sources of Morality and Religion* (1932), Bergson extended his philosophy of vitalism to the realms of morality, religion, and art.[34] As in his earlier studies, Bergson posited polar opposites—the static and the dynamic—as providing a fundamental insight into discerning dimensions of life. Here, Bergson posited two discernible moralities, or, rather, two sources: the one having its roots in intelligence, leading also to science and its static, mechanistic ideal; the other based on intuition, finding its expression not only in the free creativity of art and philosophy but also in the mystical experience of the saints.[35] Thus, in the moral, social, and religious life of humanity, Bergson recognized, on the one hand, the work of the closed society, expressed in conformity to codified laws and customs, and, on the other side, the open society, best represented by the dynamic aspirations of heroes and mystical saints reaching out beyond and even breaking the strictures of the groups in which they live. Bergsonian mysticism was illuminating for its day in that it evoked the experience and language of transcendence—artists, philosophers, saints, so inspired by such creativity, experiencing the unity of all things—and expressed itself in a call to universal love, as befitting dynamic religion and morality.

NEO-VITALISM AND CONTEMPORARY RELIGIOUS NATURALISM

References to a life force, *Lebensphilosophie*, or a vital principle virtually disappeared from scientific discourse in the early twentieth century, eradicated by sophisticated scientific explanations of the origins of life that culminated in mid-twentieth-century genetics. In the wake of Bergsonian philosophy, however, vitalism played a major role in some early twentieth-century European intellectual developments, spreading well beyond professional science into the worlds of culture and art. Some forms of vitalist art, for example, exemplified modernism's ties to

Romanticism, to post-Darwinian debates about evolution and religion, and to evolving categories of modernist spirituality and its relationship to aesthetics.[36] These developments were part of a renewed upsurge in religious thought and holistic science—particularly in England and Germany—that extensively rejected a perceived Victorian materialism.

Although the apparent contradictions that life posed to an ordered (mechanistic) universe were no longer the primary concern of biologists who articulated scientific foundations for vitalism, such conceptual issues preoccupied philosophers and religionists seeking a metaphysical grounding for their ideas. Those interested in constructing comprehensive schemes inclusive of scientific insights were thus faced with either accepting pluralism (thereby rejecting vitalistic notions) or formulating some principle of activity that would necessarily be the same in relation to both matter and life. Attempts to formulate the latter helped usher in modern process thought. Indeed, a vitalistic impetus was evident in process metaphysicians who began to articulate a view of the entire universe, including, for many, a conception of divine reality, as in a constant state of change. The term "process" was used to describe the particular kind of change, and, according to this view, process is universal activity understood as a continuity of antecedents and consequences brought about by an interrelation between true diversity and true unity.

In the twenty-first century, Western scholars are developing new premises regarding nature that evoke the key metaphors of process thought. Instead of seeing nature as immutably ordered, and change within it simply as rearrangement, thinkers now conceive of nature as evolutionary, dynamic, and emergent. Historicity is viewed as a basic attribute of nature, and science itself as being historically conditioned. In place of full determinism, scientists speak of a complex combination of law and chance, in fields as diverse as quantum physics, thermodynamics, chaos theory, and biological evolution. Both structure and openness are now understood to characterize nature. Accordingly, in a gesture that resonates with contemporary articulations of otherness, humanists are beginning to propose the image of nature as a community—an evolving, multileveled network of interdependent beings. Finally, while it may be true that today there are no self-proclaimed vitalists (at least not in the scientific world) in the manner of Driesch and Bergson, the antireductionism associated with vitalism persists, representing a crux of developments in modern science. For example, as biology and medicine continue to make strident inroads into the very substance of life, with advances in molecular biology and genetics, a form of transmuted vitalism (organismic biology) has emerged. Alternatively known as systems approach in biology, the doctrine of organismic or holistic philosophy has gained enormous strength from a number of recent advances, denying categorically the need to posit any separate energy field and also maintaining that the organic relationships between the different parts of an organism are wholly immanent in the physical structure of that living organic system.[37]

Organicism in biology resists the desire to reduce life to the bare and minimal essentials of physics and chemistry, asserting that an integrated life form is greater than the sum of its parts. Advocates of this position often differ drastically from traditional vitalists, however, in assessing how, or in what sense exactly the whole is more than the sum of its parts. While organismic biologists maintain that the additional ingredient is the understanding of 'organization' or organizing relations, humanistically oriented vitalists often assert that some non-physical entity, force or field, must be added to the laws of physics and chemistry to understand life.[38] Conway's mystical vision of sentient nature moving toward goodness anticipated some of these later developments and debates, helping to forge a conceptual space for the emergence of process religious naturalism. In the next chapter, I explore these ideas further, outlining discernible, often faint reverberations of Conway's vitalistic themes within certain twentieth-century process philosophical and theological veins.

CHAPTER 5

Processing Conway's Religious Naturalism

The imagination loses vitality as it ceases to adhere to what is real. When it adheres to the unreal and intensifies what is unreal, while its first effect may be extraordinary, that effect is the maximum effect that it will ever have.

—Wallace Stevens, *The Necessary Angel*

Conway counts among those figures in Western thought that integrated religious, scientific, and philosophical ideas while advancing a particular view of nature. Such synthesizing tendencies were vividly expressed in her explorations of ancient philosophies, in her embracing of Quaker experiential mysticism, and in her critical engagement with the new mechanical philosophy. Conway coalesced these various forms of knowledge into a religious naturalism that conceived and celebrated nature's movement toward goodness, anticipating later veins of religious naturalism in the twentieth century. In her early modern work, Conway also emphasized a key metaphor (relationality) to describe the fundamental truths of life, thus foreshadowing a particular feature that preoccupies contemporary process theorists. While Conway cannot be labeled a process thinker per se, her understanding of processual nature certainly has interesting points of convergence with process thought, lending support to the view that reverberations of her basic vitalistic thrust continue in new and fascinating forms.

CONWAY'S RELIGIOUS NATURALISM AND
TWENTIETH-CENTURY PROCESS THOUGHT

Modern process thought emerged in the early twentieth century, yet its antecedents reach as far back as some pre-Socratic philosophies. Its development also owes as much to Conway and the vitalists of the seventeenth century as it does to such later theorists as Charles S. Pierce, Francis H. Bradley, Henri Bergson, and Alfred N. Whitehead. All of these figures, in some form or another, challenged the primacy of scientific theories of mechanistic and deterministic interpretations of causality as adequate or full explanations of natural phenomena. Contemporary process thought represents a confluence of philosophic insights aimed at dismantling scientific optimism, which has escalated into a secular form of apocalyptic fulfillment. Process metaphysics diametrically opposes the general view that subordinates processes to substantial things, or denies them altogether. In a process conceptual framework, events, and relationships—rather than separate substances or separate particles—constitute reality.

Moreover, process thinkers argue that the notion of material substance expresses a useful abstraction for many purposes of life and has a sound pragmatic defense, yet sole reliance on such ontology yields a deficient and impoverished view of reality. This seductive lure of abstraction encourages self-deception and illusory ideations, allowing abstractions from reality to pass for reality itself. As stated by Alfred N. Whitehead, "This error does not consist in the employment of the word 'substance'; but in the employment of the notion of an actual entity which is characterized by essential qualities, and remains numerically one amidst the changes of accidental relations and of accidental qualities."[1]

In process metaphysical systems, becoming, not being, is the central metaphor for understanding reality, and contingency, emergence, and creativity are essential elements that take precedence over determinism and fixity. Process thought encourages us to take very seriously the actuality of change; accordingly, nothing is constant, everything is in flux. This idea resonates with Bergson's earlier observation that "reality appears as a ceaseless upspringing of something new, which has no sooner arisen to make the present than it has already fallen back into the past."[2] Rejecting the dominant ontology, which posits reality as material substance, static, and non-experiencing, process metaphysicians often characterize reality as processional, dynamic, and capable of experience. In a process conceptual framework, for example, all processes have an objective nature (i.e., processes can be experienced by subjects), a subjective nature (i.e., processes can experience, are partly self-determining, and can enter into relation with other processes), and a temporal nature (i.e., processes happen through time or, perhaps, define time).

In the early twentieth century, Whitehead offered a remarkably innovative picture of reality in which the basic unit of nature is not static material substance, but rather creative, experiential events, actual occasions of experience. In his classic cosmological work, *Process and Reality* (1929), Whitehead posited the building blocks of reality as "actual occasions" or processional units, with human experience showing the most supreme exemplification of these living units of elemental experience.[3] In the language of Whitehead, complex objects are societies, or nexus, of actual occasions that endure cooperatively. Complex objects are no mere aggregates, but possess a defining unity. Enduring material substance is mere appearance and exists as the stable patterns established by sequential processes. Process philosophy justifies all of these claims on the existential grounds that we can only truly understand the units constituting the physical world by analogy with our own experience that we know from within.

The Whiteheadian system thus acknowledges a new sort of relationship between experience and consciousness. All actual entities, and not just conscious beings, enjoy experience: "Consciousness presupposes experience, and not experience consciousness."[4] Stated another way, this means that we must look within, see the experiences of our life, and understand that they are not things that happen to us, but rather are the fundamental elements of the real that comprise us. We are our experiences and we change without ceasing. Furthermore, in a Whiteheadian processional framework, there is also a dynamic relationship between individual organisms. The technical term "internal relations" helps us make sense of these activities.[5] Basic unit-events of the world are not vacuous, but rather possess a subjective nature that allows them attributes that might be called feeling, memory, and creativity. Every event, while influenced by the past through a process Whitehead calls prehension, exercises some amount of self-determination or self-creation. Each occurrence in turn exerts influence, which enters into the becoming of other occurrences. The potential of each event to exert creative influence on the future characterizes the creative advance into novelty, which is a key feature of Whitehead's cosmos.

In Conway's religious cosmology, similar features of natural processes, suggestive of a dynamic, evolving view of reality, are found—albeit expressed in early modern idiom. For instance, Conway's conceptual worldview also contains a network of interactions of events or actual occasions (she called them spiritual particles or monads) that are interdependent. Additionally, the pivotal notion "prehension" in Whitehead's theory, which indicates precisely the point of "internal relations" between and among actual entities, is discernible in Conway's schema.[6] In other words, Conway's particles (monads) seem to resemble Whitehead's actual occasions in terms of prehending what goes on around them in a way that encompasses a low-grade mode of emotion, consciousness, and purpose. Moreover, the ethical and ecological perspectives that are richly suggestive in Conway's religious philosophy are more fully explicit in Whitehead's cosmology. An emphasis on internal relations as constitutive of all individual entities in the universe leads to the Whiteheadian notion that all events are literally members one of another. This aesthetic, ethical vision of nature is what Conway was suggesting in her own novel way when she formulated the fundamental ethical mandate for all of nature to love each other.[7] In Whitehead, as in Conway, microcosm and macrocosm are coordinated, linked to one another in a seamless web of process. There is also a dialectical tension between individual and world—each item of existence in nature touches the others and without them would not be what it is. Finally, Conway's depiction of all creatures perfecting themselves in the participation of goodness resembles one of Whitehead's earliest views that all livings things are characterized by a threefold urge: to live, to live well, and to live better.[8]

Whitehead and Conway's shared conviction that natural processes experience a dynamic urging toward fuller transformation also finds innovative expression in the work of another twentieth-century process thinker, Henry Nelson Wieman. More specifically, Wieman's philosophy of creative interchange resonates with Conway's aesthetic-ethical vision of nature, showing further reverberations across the centuries. I believe this is the case for two general reasons. First, Wieman advanced a theological empirical process that continues the tradition of value discourse on nature inaugurated by Conway. In Wieman's theory of creativity and creative exchange, one finds a religious impulse that challenges the dominant tradition of morally disengaged scientific discourse about nature. What Conway described as the constitutive vital movements of creation becomes translatable by Wieman as the impetus of all life toward love, justice, and right relationships. Both thinkers simultaneously incorporated and rejected aspects of influential scientific cosmologies while advancing aesthetic, ethical visions of nature.

Second, two hundred years after Conway explored a vitalist metaphysics expressing a continuum of relations from the divine to the most inconspicuous form of matter, we find Wieman emphasizing relationality as one of the most fundamental truths of life. He, too, in his own way, celebrated events and relationships rather than reality as separate substances or particles. In distinct ways, each thinker proposed an organismic metaphysics in which experience, feeling, power, and potentiality are key categories characterizing the whole and the parts. In advancing these qualities, both Conway and Wieman were primarily concerned to show the importance of humans' relationships to other natural processes as well as to divine reality. In both of their conceptual formulations, a matrix of relationships occurs in which all of natural processes participate in divine life through concretizing divine love and through perfecting self and each other. Yet, as I will explain later in more detail, while Wieman's process framework may reverberate with some of Conway's early modern concerns, his theistic framework harbored an intriguing empirical bent that Conway did not conceive during her time.

HENRY NELSON WIEMAN'S RELIGIOUS PHILOSOPHY OF CREATIVE INTERCHANGE

In the early thirties in the United States, Wieman's empirical theism was primarily concerned with the character of God as verified by the existential medium, that is, the sphere in which we live, move, and have our being. According to Wieman, most contemporary views of God were inadequate because they presented ideas about beliefs in God, instead of ideas deriving from experiences of God. Religious commitment, he felt, should be to the experienced reality of God and not to a mere concept: "The word 'God' should refer to what actually operates to save and not merely to some belief about what operates in this way. But in current usage the word actually refers to pictures in the mind and not to the actuality."[9] For Wieman, the conceptions of deity espoused by influential theologians touted a rationalism that was shorn of the facticity that an empirically based theology could claim.

Wieman felt that a particular method must be followed before one could gain knowledge of God, or any knowledge at all. In his early works, he called this method the scientific method, the empirical method, the method of reason, or even the common sense method.

This process involved, for Wieman, basic observations regarding the functional and operative meaning of creativity. In these earlier writings, the observation of certain experiences was based on sensory data and intuition. For Wieman, it was not the individual, however, who produced these experiences. They were instead products of a transformative power, God, which gave particular form or character to the given context. For Wieman, God creates by giving a direction of value to a particular process of becoming. Divine creativity works through the development of culture as it centers on a particular situation, in order to transform the situation into a salvific experience.

An important shift in Wieman's thought occurred during the thirties and forties, and it is this phase of his work, I believe, that has most potential resonance with Conway's religious naturalism. The imagery in Wieman's writings of this time reflected his growing sensitivity to social concerns and threats to human survival. After World War II and Hiroshima, Wieman's theological writings became oriented toward a wider cultural situation. This new emphasis led him to a fuller interpretation of God within a philosophy of creativity. Wieman's continued interest in creativity showed forth prominently in *Normative Psychology of Religion* (1935), which offers an analysis of supreme value as "that connection between enjoyable activities by which they support one another, enhance one another, and, at a higher level, mean one another."[10] This work shows that value does not lie in the events themselves, but rather in the connection of these events. Value, hence, is interpreted as the combination of "what is" and "what may be"—a combination of actuality and possibility. When one gains meaning from the connections, value occurs in such a way that there is growth of value.

The increase of value in the functional connection between activities should not be identified with universal programs; it only means that within the scope of the conditions under consideration there is an increase of growth. It sums up all that can be hoped for in terms of the best conceivable world. Growth of meaning describes the creative process (identified as God) by which the enhancement of the world takes place through the enhancement of its individual members. This supreme value is superhuman, but not supernatural. The distinction is that it is not something wholly outside of human life ("supernatural"), but it does operate beyond the plans and visions of individuals ("superhuman"), bringing forth values humans cannot foresee, and often developing connections of mutual support and mutual meaning in spite of, or contrary to, the efforts of humans.[11]

In *The Source of Human Good* (1946), his most important work, Wieman furthered his analysis of creative value within the context of human interactions and purposeful living. He appeared even more intent on addressing the empirical happenings of creative value—how valuing occurs concretely and dynamically within the lived experience of people—and identifying specific occurrences expressive of it. In the text, Wieman identifies God as the source of human good, asserting that human good can be increased only by progressive accumulation of good through a sequence of generations; a further suggestion is that this good cannot accumulate so long as humans are preoccupied with seeking only the material goods of life.

A key phrase in this book is "the creative event," a highly complex concept connoting creativity as operating in human life to give it qualitative meaning. Notably, in the text, creativity is not merely identified with the common usages often associated with it. For example, creativity is not solely associated with innovative behavior on the part of individuals, nor as achievements produced by imaginative and artistic persons (though these would be included as instances of it). Rather, the creative event describes a process of reorganizing the many discordant parts of our lives into a more inclusive whole. The divine reality is creativity, in the sense that God is the character, structure, or form that enables the events of human life to be creative. Humanity's creative ability is something produced in us as a consequence of the prior workings of the creative event. Wieman identifies the creative event not merely with the work of God, but with the being of God. He uses the term "being" to convey the idea that this event is a concrete reality embracing four unified but distinct subevents. Briefly stated, they are:

1. the emerging awareness of qualitative meaning through communication;

2. the integration of these new meanings with those previously acquired;

3. the expanding of quality in the appreciable world;

4. the widening and deepening of community.[12]

The first event is the primary context from which the other three emerge. For Wieman, a stream of experience comes to us first as qualitative immediacy and then becomes cognized into knowledge relations. In other words, qualitative meaning occurs when every organism reacts so as to break the passage of existence into units or intervals called "events" and to relate these to one another. Thus, when a single organism is able to acquire the qualitative meanings developed by other organisms and add them to its own, the human mind and its appreciable world are transformed. Events include within their structures possibilities for development. Qualities, or values, are the things of which events are made. They are the ontological reality of an event: "Every event accessible to human experience is a quality or complex of qualities; also, every event is an instance of energy."[13] Further, a "conjunction" is a new or more complex event made up of a strand of events. When a conjunction occurs in such a way that the qualities of the event included in the conjunction fulfill their possibilities to a greater degree, there is an increase of meaning, or qualitative meaning.

According to the logic of Wieman's thought, the events cannot foresee the developments possible to them, nor can the universe determine whether there will be an increase or decrease of value. There must be some determining factor responsible for integrating the values of the individual events. This one factor is God, for it is the process of progressive integration of value within the universe. Accordingly, God reveals Godself to us in events in such a way that we can understand and learn how to bring forth conditions that allow for an increase of value. As the creative event, God is the highest value. God is part of the cosmic whole, but at the same time is not to be simply identified with the universe. Limitations are placed on God by the present realities at hand. In other words, God can only work with what is present. The knowledge gained through this interaction is a good example of Wieman's epistemological basis: "The creative event as treated here includes only those events which bring a new structure whereby the human mind distinguishes and relates events in such a way that there is more richness of quality in happenings as they occur and greater range and variety of appreciated possibility."[14] The creative event is unknowable aside from the way it functions in relation to other events.

VITAL REVERBERATIONS: COMPARING CONWAY AND WIEMAN'S RELIGIOUS NATURALISMS

Wieman's religious naturalism, or his philosophy of creative interchange, can be a interpreted as a later model of vitalistic philosophy in two ways: (1) as a later detranscendentalizing religious vitalism that is distinct among classical and other foundationalist "modern" forms of religious thinking; and (2) as a materially based hermeneutic that challenges the linguistic authority of current postmodern theory, much of which has fostered historical abstractions or a sterile aestheticism devoid of ethical charges and material force. The first point becomes apparent when juxtaposing Wieman and Conway's perspectives on the movement of natural processes within distinct theistic frameworks. For both, the proper focus of nature's movement toward goodness is ascertaining the divine source or explanation for such life or movement in organisms. However, as we have seen, Conway's articulation of a vital force, "an energy force," that created nature partakes in, is, in the last analysis, necessarily something that is derived from a divine transcendence that resides beyond the natural world. In the context of seventeenth-century rationalism, Conway's conceptualization of divinity is a "freestanding thing" in itself, not the effect of some causal process. Although natural creatures, constituted of monads, actualize this divine force in relational processional movements toward perfection, there still remains an incommensurable gap between divine nature and the rest of nature.[15] In Conway's conceptual monism, the divine has a qualitative, distinct nature that resists complete identification with processional, created nature, protecting her early modern mind against charges of pantheism.

Wieman's process theism is quite different from Conway's more traditional supernatural theism of classical theology. From his perspective, the divine source or explanation for life in organisms is inherent in the natural world, not transcendent or supernatural. In the opening chapters of *The Source of Human Good,* Wieman clearly rejects the transcendental, ahistorical, nonsensual affirmations celebrated within the dominant Christian theological tradition: "Thus the active God derived from the Jewish tradition and the Forms derived from the Greek tradition are both brought down into the world of space, time, and matter and are there identified as events displaying a definite structure with possibilities."[16] Wieman's theism is understood and described in terms of God's function. Although human need forms the basis from which this function is delineated, the stress is on the remarkable creativity that can be both discernible and elusive to reasoning individuals. And although his view of God as creativity does not totally rid itself of the residue of philosophic idealism, Wieman's pragmatism and his scientific emphasis tend to avoid the subtle rationalism that characterizes much process cosmology. Their fundamental metaphysical orientations, notwithstanding, Wieman's and Conway's discourses on nature show the continuity and transformations of vitalist discourse in religious thought over the last two hundred years.

This insight leads to my second point, namely, that despite their basic differences in characterizing divine nature, Wieman's empirically

oriented processional worldview and Conway's rationalist-based processional cosmology reveal implicit ethical principles and assumptions
that are inherently anti-exploitative and capable of inspiring our com-
mitments and shaping our lives. Conway's subjectivism of nature
evokes an aesthetic-ethical force to the natural world. Her naturalistic
metaphysical system includes certain principles that may help shape
and inform human nature's behaviors in its relational movement toward actualization. Among these are:

1. Emphasis on the life of all things as expressions of a life force.

2. Rejection of a radical dualism of matter and spirit.

3. Acceptance of an immanent activity permeating nature.

4. Reverence for the goodness inherent in all creation.

5. Recognition of a universal love among all "forms" of nature.[17]

All of these principles involve an understanding of love as a symbol of immanentist, vital interactions among all natural processes. Avoiding abstract and sterile articulations of love, Conway's religious
philosophy in *The Principles* seeks transformation of self, of world, and
of neighbor through the metaphor of relational love. In it, divinity dwells
in love, first and foremost, and bestows such upon all of created nature:
"But there is yet another reason for love, when beings which love each
other are not one substance, but one has given being to another and is
the genuine and real cause of it. So it is between God and the creatures.
For he gave existence, life, and motion to everything and he therefore
loves everything and is unable not to love everything."[18] As I discussed
in the first part, Conway saw this expression of divine love expressed
in Quaker mysticism as well as in esoteric wisdoms, especially the
Lurianic Kabbalah. Although most of Conway's seventeenth-century
contemporaries shared her belief in the necessity of deity as the source
of life, very few members of her social class interpreted the divine life
and its transformations of creation as extensively as she did, as evinced
in the responses of More to Conway's conversion to Quakerism and to
her fascination with certain esoteric doctrines.

Centuries later, in a very different cultural context, Wieman's
empirical process model reverberates with Conway's pragmatic and
communal orientations of divine love's efficacy in the universe. One
implication of Wieman's thought is that human beings receive both
freedom and the potentiality of creative community through creative
interchange or communication. This possibility for transformation is

given to humans through two sources, a primary one and a secondary one. The primary source is creativity as creative interchange—this is identified as the "transforming actuality," better known as God. The secondary source is what human beings can learn to do by providing the right conditions for release of creative interchange in human existence, individually and collectively. When this secondary source is disconnected and alienated from the primary source, it becomes merely a moral effort and not an authentic religious commitment to the primary source. It is the responsibility of humans to open ourselves to creative interchange as the source of good in order that we may be "saved." Here a persistent mystical strand in both Wieman's and Conway's thought appears, namely, that humans cannot fully actualize ourselves through our own creative efforts: creative interchange is not a pseudonym for simple humanistic morality.

In a later chapter of *The Source of Human Good,* Wieman introduces the notion of the "perceptual event" as contributing to what is observable in the acquisition of knowledge of God. The perceptual event includes everything within and around the biological organism, which experimentation demonstrates as making a difference to conscious awareness when perceptual reaction occurs.[19] Observable experience is transformed into a God-experience when cultural imagery and sensibilities and historical conditionings converge with the experience at hand, yielding value or meaning within the present event. The present event thus becomes interpreted and validated within a larger communal context. This activity, in turn, results in a greater sense of possibilities for the future through the enhancement of others and oneself, which is another way of asserting that knowledge of God is attained. In the Wiemanian context, God alone accounts for the possibilities for new meanings and new values in human existence. Creativity is God operating in human existence to create wider and deeper community of shared values between individuals and peoples, while expanding the valuing consciousness of each participant individual. Such an aesthetic vision has some affinity to Conway's cosmological views, as expressed in the following words: "There is a certain divine law and instinct with which he has endowed all rational creatures so that they love him, which is the fulfillment of all the commandments."[20]

In "Technical Postscript to the Source of Human Good," Wieman expands on his naturalistic metaphysics, outlining important features of the creative event. Creativity is identified as the character, structure, or form that the event must have to be creative. Creativity is an abstraction, whereas the concrete reality is now designated as the "creative event." The creative event is changeless in respect to that structure whereby we call it creative, even though the concrete wholeness of the event is always changing.[21] The same can be said of other events within the universe—the universe is the basic nexus of events that contains an infinity of events. The universe is a universe only because, through-out all its changes, there is a constitutive structure whereby we call it a universe. Underlying Wieman's naturalism is the assumption that the mind and the universe are interdependent; they are appreciative and appreciable. Yet their interdependence is not an enduring identity. The universe that we experience transforms its nature according to the conditions of our bodies. Emphasis is on the interaction between the psychophysical organism and its environment, and between its sev-eral parts.[22] That reality underlying all others, in the sense of a change-less structure of felt quality and knowable order, is creativity because it is necessarily prior to every other form of experience.

With his naturalist metaphysics, Wieman also reveals the impor-tance of having a creative and liberating commitment to that ultimate reality. This deeper commitment is, again, to the actuality, and not merely to ideas about it. From Wieman's perspective, we must view our ideas critically because a deeper commitment to God delivers one from bond-age to our ideas of God. This faith commitment also entails conformity of lifestyle and behavior to the overall purpose of the creative event: the increase of human freedom, individually and collectively, as accompa-nied by growth of creative community.[23] Likewise, Conway's early modern idiom features a notion of cosmic community through the flow of participatory goodness within the created order. Conway conceptu-alizes the divine goodness as the source of all apparent goodness found in each instant of created goodness, which, in turn, compels an ethical response to such expansive relationality: "But if one maintains that there is yet another reason for love, which is the principal one, namely, good-ness, which is the strongest attraction of love and the reason why God must be loved as much as possible by all things because he is the best, then where there is also such goodness, either real or apparent, in his creatures, their fellow creatures love them."[24]

Wieman also reiterates Conway's thesis concerning the notion of organic and primordial interrelatedness among all organisms. For Conway, the love among all creation constitutes a sacral universe where the shared love among all entities is based on a processional view of natural phenomena participating in the divine life. Likewise, for Wieman, the transformation of individuals comes about through inter-action with others. A healthy encounter with others helps to promote the possibility of creative community. The isolated person can never experience God, or so it seems. Wieman's naturalism relies on a compelling vision of interrelatedness, organic growth, and mutual support and meaning for all that participate in the processes of creativity.

This focus on relationality, or active, creative interactions among fundamental events, emphasizes Wieman's uncompromising affirmation of the material base of reality; it is a point of emphasis that confounds both traditional Western metaphysical systems and the purely aesthetic (or "first wave") veins of postmodernism that have recently come under attack. For example, Wieman's method presupposes an active, concrete reality (the creative event) that participates in and helps sustain creativity within human experience. With the use of the faculties—which involve rational analysis, observation, intuition, and so on—the individual is granted opportunities to gain knowledge of this reality. An important point here is that we come with our whole being to know and to respond to that "Something" that saves us from isolation and illusions.

For Wieman, the ultimate determination of truth and knowledge is the creative event generating the rational principles of the mind and the structure of matter in mutual determination of each other. In addition, this progressive creativity produces a culture that shapes the reactions of the human body, the direction of attentive consciousness, and technology, so that empirical findings will yield reliable knowledge inductively established within this framework of order shared in common by the mind and its appreciable world.[25] The appeal of such an arrangement, as I see it, is the orientation of the entire, concrete, embodied subject in apprehending what could be designated as creativity at work in the universe. Most notably, Wieman's conception of (ultimate) reality is materially based, where matter is conceived as a form of energy that determines the very structure of time and space, together with all else that exists or is possible.

Wieman's vitalistic orientations differ from Conway's in this specific area of ascertaining the interplay of differences and unity in the cosmos. For Conway, everything in the created order has the potential to contribute to certain inhabitable worlds of goodness as nature perfects itself in movement toward the essential goodness that is the foundation of all life. Most interesting, Conway's monistic tendencies, expressed in her published text, correlate with an all-inclusive orientation in her intellectual queries and in her religious quest. Her deployment of discourses that often seem disconnected bears some similarity to the seventeenth-century poetic trope of the metaphysical conceit, based on the notion of "concordia discord," or harmony amid discord. Conway's formulation of a monistic system is rhetorically sophisticated, borrowing from various discourses that act as a sort of poetic cataloguing or list. In addressing nature, it serves first as a Homeric catalogue explaining the plenitude, finally appropriating discordant items to emphasize monastic unity. Wieman's naturalistic framework, on the other hand, demonstrates that what was once viewed as unitary is actually constituted by a plurality; certainties are seen as ambiguities; and univocal simplicities are unmasked as complexities. Wieman's description of how growth of meaning may occur also challenges the popular notion of guaranteed theoretical progress, which is a trap of the modernist paradigm, strongly influenced by a logic of thesis, antithesis, and synthesis.

Most notably, even with its emphasis on the structure of the creative event, Wieman's religious naturalism foreshadowed important poststructuralist insights regarding the open-endedness of our practices and struggles, and the fact that we live in worlds of paradox and uncertainty. In it, Wieman seems to have rejected modernism's triumphalism or love affair with guaranteed progress: "Perhaps the human organism does not have the nervous energy and capacity for diversified and complex feeling that is required to enter appreciatively into the riches of other races and cultures in a manner necessary to avoid destructive conflict."[26] Although it appears that Wieman aimed to conceive of the whole, a careful, critical reading of his various writings yields a poststructuralist historiography that resists the lure of totalism. His religious functionalism, I contend, prevents Wieman from sliding into rationalist purity or theological totalism. As he asserts, "[F]inal outcomes, as well as all original beginnings, are entirely beyond the scope of our knowing."[27] Granted, Wieman conceives of the creative event as changeless, unified, absolutely good, and eternal in respect to its creativity. But, as noted earlier, this event also displays change, multiplicity, and temporality. As he closes *The Source of Human Good*, Wieman maintains:

> We must say of this metaphysics, as we said of our interpretation of value, that it is not the only true one. There are several metaphysics, all of which are true, because a metaphysics is true if it selects some element necessarily involved in all human existence and explains everything in terms of it. . . . The metaphysics of creativity herein developed is chosen in preference to any other because we believe it provides a better guide to action than any other.[28]

These words demonstrate a unique feature of Wieman's thought that is not readily gleaned from other process systems: there is no single truth, but rather, at best, more or less comprehensive and convincing versions of truth that carry with them particular social implications. This is also a necessarily crucial difference between Conway's early modern idiom and Wieman's later modern one. In different periods, and with different theistic orientations, Conway and Wieman contributed to a visionary trajectory of thought that inspires contemporary Westerners to create egalitarian systems of relationality, replacing those systems requiring asymmetrical and imbalanced forms of authority, power, and control. With an uncompromising affirmation of the fuller view of reality, they offered compelling visions of interrelatedness, organic growth, mutual support, and meaning for all that participate in processes of becoming.

The sketchy comparison of Conway and Wieman that I have given illustrates, at the least, sympathetic vibrations across the centuries; it also demonstrates that a fundamental philosophical struggle was going on in early modernity between ways of comprehending our connections with each other and with all of nature. The trajectory of religious naturalism initiated by Conway, and exemplified most recently by process cosmologies, encourages contemporary religionists to accept a quintessential ethical task for our age: continued reflection on our evolving nature. In the final chapter, I elaborate on this theme as I examine reverberations of Conway's vitalism in aspects of feminist religious discourse.

CHAPTER 6

Cultural Reverberations

Love, Religious Naturalism, and Feminism

We live in all we seek. The hidden shows up in too-plain sight. It lives captive on the face of the obvious—the people, events, and things of the day—to which we as sophisticated children have long since become oblivious. What a hideout: Holiness lies spread and borne over the surface of time and stuff like color.

—Annie Dillard, *For the Time Being*

When the concept of nature is divorced from such qualities as love, truth, beauty, goodness, and all other perceived values, it loses the capacity to inspire, to guide, or to help humans experience fuller dimensions of life. Conway understood this important insight in the seventeenth century. Although critical of the new mechanical science, she did not reject it; nor did she fully divorce mechanistic theories from religious and philosophical truths, or, more generally, from the search for meaning and value. Rather, Conway suggested that there was more to nature than the mechanical operations described by Descartes and others. She preferred to speak of the intrinsic vital movements of processional nature, of an experience of interiority beyond the scope of gross functionalism captured by mechanism.

Conway's conceptualization of nature conveyed more than its functional and descriptive aspects, featuring such important values as

goodness and love. With other vitalists of her era, she believed important religious and philosophical perspectives would be lost if the reductionistic premises of the mechanistic worldview were advanced
without explicit reference to the sacredness of all natural processes or
sentient entities. Conway's suspicions were not unfounded—combined
with mechanical conceptualizations, the new science, which was institutionalized by learned societies with royal support, helped justify an
instrumentalist treatment of certain forms of nature, leading to the
exclusion of nonhuman nature from ethical significance in modernity.
Moreover, restoration science achieved a new system of investigation
that unified material power with knowledge.

Bacon's *The New Organon* (1620) helped set the stage for these
desacralizing movements.[1] Social, economic, and political forces shaped
the set of purportedly objective, neutral scientific procedures inaugurated by Bacon and others. Granted, Bacon designed his program of
scientific research to benefit society at large; his appeal to empirical
investigation contained the implicitly egalitarian principle that all
persons could verify the truth for themselves. However, in his mechanistic utopia, *The New Atlantis* (1624), Bacon uncritically accepted his
period's gender and class stratifications that supported social inequality in seventeenth-century English culture.[2] Although Bacon is not solely
responsible for seventeenth-century conceptualizations validating the
woman/nature relationship or for later adaptations of his philosophy
of nature, his scientific metaphors and program certainly aided a
mechanistic worldview in which "disorderly, active nature was soon
forced to submit to the questions and experimental techniques of the
new science. . . . Female imagery became a tool in adapting scientific
knowledge and method to a new form of human power over nature."[3]

Unfortunately, scientific developments in the eighteenth and nineteenth centuries continued to employ power-laden constructions of
nature, which frequently correlated with patterns of gender and racial
injustice. In the field of medicine, for example, the eighteenth-century
Montpellier vitalists advanced some problematic perspectives on the
nature and role of women. As I indicated earlier, their vitalist principles challenged the body machine metaphor introduced by Descartes,
and maintained an important distinction between living, organized
being and brute, inert matter. They also helped introduce a medical
discourse that subtlety challenged the progress, optimism, and universalism that undergird Enlightenment discourses of domination.

These French vitalists envisioned inexhaustive interactions of internal dispositions and external milieu that led to distinctive human
types formed by age, sex, temperament, region, and other forces. How-

ever, while attempting to describe and honor the distinctive vital forces in women, these physicians helped perpetuate the cult of domesticity that relegated women to the private sphere. They introduced a moral element in medical discourse that, in practice, "proved peculiarly manipulable by self-styled expert 'observers' who asserted the exclusive authority to judge what was full and what was deficient, what was conducive to vital 'harmony' and what was discordant; what, finally, was normal and pathological."[4] Pierre Roussel's 1775 treatise on women, for instance, insisted that women differed from men in general constitution and temperament, as well as in other bodily features (e.g., bones, nerves, muscles, and blood). Roussel's theory was based on the vitalist principle that the human organism was constituted by energies distributed throughout the body's centers, eventually expended in one direction or function. In establishing this theory, Roussel believed women retained much of their childhood characteristics, which men lost as they developed muscles, animal force, and strength:

> Advancing toward puberty woman seems to distance herself less than does man from her original constitution. Delicate and tender, she retains forever something of the temperament proper to children. The texture of her organs loses nothing of its original softness; the developments that age produces in all the parts of her body do not give the same degree of consistency as in man. . . . Although she departs from the same point as man, she develops a manner proper to her alone so that, arrived at a certain age, she finds . . . that she is provided with new attributes and is subject to an order of functions foreign to man and up to that point unknown to herself.[5]

Later, in the nineteenth century, English scientific notions about gender differences often presented inequalities of rights between the sexes as reflecting prescripts of nature. Scientists of all sorts intervened in the Woman Question—the issue of the nature of women and their roles in society. As the decoders of nature, these scientists often claimed the official role as arbiters of social change, contributing to the various debates about the natural aptitudes and capacities of the sexes and their ensuing social roles.[6] Aligning women with the domestic sphere and men with the public domain, evolutionists like George Romanes defended physiologically based "natural" differences. Romanes asserted that maternal instincts, the strongest of all influences in the determination of character, made women naturally more nurturing, less competitive, and more moral than men.[7] He also asserted that anatomical and physiological considerations prohibited *a priori* any argument for the natural equality of the sexes.

Charles Darwin was another major contributor to the debates on the Woman Question, introducing another layer of complexity to the construction of gender in scientific discourses. His *Descent of Man, and Selection in Relation to Sex* emerged as an important authoritative source for those seeking a biological basis for understanding physical and mental distinctions between the sexes.[8] According to Darwin, differences between the sexes were constituted by primary sexual features (or the reproductive organs) and by secondary sexual characters, or those differences between the sexes that were not directly connected to the act of reproduction. For Darwin, these secondary sexual characters had developed through sexual and natural selection.

Darwin's theory asserted that males had become ultimately superior to females, and were stronger and larger than women, because the most dominant and daring men had succeeded best in the general struggle for life, as well as in securing wives, thus leaving a large number of offspring.[9] While Darwin believed civilization had diminished male combat for mates, he maintained that sexual selection, which dates back to primeval times, continued to specific human mental powers such as intelligence and morality. In Darwin's schema, women were stronger in morality, men in intellect:

> Woman seems to differ from man in mental disposition, chiefly in her greater tenderness and less selfishness. Man is the rival of other men; he delights in competition. . . . It is generally admitted that with woman the powers of intuition, of rapid perception, and perhaps of imitation, are more strongly marked than in man; but some, at least, of these faculties are characteristic of the lower races, therefore of a past and lower state of civilization. The chief distinction in the intellectual powers of the two sexes is shown by man's attaining to a higher eminence, in whatever he takes up, than can woman—whether requiring deep thought, reason, or imagination, or merely the use of the senses and hands.[10]

Darwin's ideas contained troubling gender and racial assumptions, which helped to validate and perpetuate various forms of human subjugation. His views generally reflected nineteenth-century Victorian ideals and were more enthusiastically received than those of John Stuart Mill, who proposed in "The Subjection of Women" that female characteristics were not innate.[11] The warm reception to his views was due, in large part, to the dominant cultural conception that the natural aptitudes of classes of people formed the basis for their social roles.

Other disturbing social and cultural effects of modern science were evident in scientific uses of vitalistic principles, such as belief in evolution as teleology, which helped promote Enlightenment racism. Georges-Louis Leclerc Comte de Buffon's *Histoire Naturelle* (1749–67), for instance, connected the marriage of "superior" races and "inferior" ones to degeneracy.[12] This view came to fruition in the full-blown racism of Count Gobnineau's 1853 *The Inequality of Human Races* and Houston Chamberlain's 1899 *The Principles of the Nineteenth Century*.[13] Furthermore, in the nineteenth century, scientific studies of race were aided by such activities as phrenology, along with developments in comparative anatomy, physiology, histology, and paleontology—all assisting in establishing the classification of human racial differences as innate, primordial, and permanent. By the 1890s, the concept of race had become the major organizing principle for developments in the life and human sciences, where "a growing belief in materialism, that life could be explained by matter in motion without resorting to vital spirits or a notion of soul, emboldened scientists to reject the Bible as the authoritative source for knowledge about nature."[14]

These scientific developments, along with specific Enlightenment conceptions of reason, sanctioned a form of Euro-Western ethnocentricity in generating theories that were taken to be universally true and socially efficacious. Collapsing differences of culture, race, and religious orientation into a uniform and Eurocentric mode of being, Enlightenment reasoning provided an ideal intellectual and epistemological basis for authorizing the hegemony of the West over against the other traditions Europeans were beginning to encounter in Asia, in Africa, and in the Americas. Scientists viewed with suspicion those traditions, values, and folk practices that were not compatible with or radically different from the Enlightenment ideal, placing them low down on the hierarchy, beneath the required level of cognition or scientificity.[15]

The ideology of the civilized and progressive West also justified some of the most savagely brutal practices imaginable, ironically, with its rhetoric of liberal humanism. Espousing the universal rights of humans—or, as it has most often been posited, the rights of [MAN]—Enlightenment discourse often spawned a distinct set of discursive formations and cultural practices that justified unjust capitalist social relations in the West and their extension, via colonialism and imperialism, to other societies.[16] The peculiar violence of this liberal universal discourse was evident in its development of the Euro-Anglo construction of "whiteness" as the normative identity for human subjectivity. This form of racism depended on a logic of racial difference whereby one group's self-definition as white became the normative standpoint for judging other groups' proximity to or distance from its idealized self-construction. Thus, the white liberal European subject often identified itself as full and others (those identified as nonwhites) as empty, or existing in the condition of lack. In modernity, the most complete and extreme form of this racialized binary logic resulted in the construction of the superiority of a 'white" race over "black" races.[17]

Afro-Caribbean postcolonial writers Frantz Fanon and Amie Cesaire offered powerful indictments of such enlightened racialized reason (or reasoned racism). Their works illustrate that, depending on who is speaking, the self-congratulatory proclamations of humanism can be quickly unmasked as fraudulent claims and violent acts of genocide. Writing to his contemporaries struggling against colonialism, Fanon advised:

> Let us waste no time in sterile litanies and nauseating mimicry. Leave this Europe where they are never done talking of Man, yet murder men everywhere they find them, at the corner of every one of their own streets, in all corners of the globe. For centuries they have stifled almost the whole of humanity in the name of a so-called spiritual experience. Look at them swaying between atomic and spiritual disintegration. . . . That same Europe where they were never done talking of Man, and where they never stopped proclaiming that they were only anxious for the welfare of Man: today we know with what sufferings humanity has paid for every one of their triumphs of the mind. . . . Come then, comrades, the European game has finally ended, we must find something different.[18]

In the twentieth-first century, various humanists are also hoping to find something different as we continue challenging impoverished and detrimental constructions of gender and racial differences produced by a modern scientific project enabled by Enlightenment instrumentalism. I also consider this an opportune moment to pause and consider the full heuristic value of Conway's work for religious humanists today. During her time, Conway challenged the dominance of the commonly accepted epistemological sources of scientific reasoning and the consequent methods used to achieve it. She boldly associated crucial values with created nature in her cosmological constructions, incorporating various forms of knowledge that were not readily accepted by the cultural elites and composers of truth of her era.

Conway's conceptual audacity invigorates religious naturalists seeking to apply philosophical and religious reflection to natural phenomenon, who are not content to let others simply describe its mechanics or operations. Her work on nature encourages some of us to engage in "world-formation," namely, to envision and to help implement new forms of relationality among all natural processes that bring about new inhabited worlds of hope and transformation. In other words, as I see it, Conway's historic example evokes a fundamental truth of religious valuing, that is, a tenacious refusal of humans to reduce our various actions to mere determinist forces and mechanistic explanations of cause/effect. During the early modern period, Conway's philosophy of vitalism attributed intrinsic value to all that exists, and it featured a vision of humanity's unique place/role/activity in a complex network of changing processes.

Important insights from Conway's religious naturalism are reverberating today, urgently, and in important ways. As my discussion in chapter 5 suggests, some of her early modern vitalistic principles resonate—in significant, albeit very different directions—with particular twentieth-century process theological and philosophical strains. In Wieman's processional view of nature, for example, humans as natural organisms help create the necessary conditions that may produce worlds of hope and goodness. In their respective systems, Wieman and Conway emphasize that humans constantly perfect themselves in processes of becoming and loving, avoiding solipsistic illusions and isolated, egotistic tendencies. Additionally, other process theorists continue to challenge a tradition of morally disengaged scientific objectivity, addressing gender and racial biases in modern constructions of "human" nature.[19]

I also detect, however faintly, aesthetic-ethical reverberations of Conway's antidualistic approach in the countertraditions of contemporary feminist thought. In the postmodern era, specific feminist trajectories have consistently, and without compromise, challenged the ill-conceived notions of gender and racial identities based on archaic dualistic philosophies and on old scientific myths; they have also questioned the persistent (and popular) view that humans stand apart from nature. In this final chapter, I trace the articulations of ecosocial principles emerging from diverse feminist discourses, demonstrating the fuller ethical import of contemporary religious naturalism. In other words, I consider how world-formation occurs in specific religious feminist discourses that accentuate the values of love and goodness formulated by Conway.

WESTERN FEMINIST DISCOURSES' CHALLENGES TO A LEGACY OF DUALISTIC THINKING

From its inception as a systematic counter discourse, Western feminism has demanded that its legitimacy be acknowledged, even as it pointed to the social constructedness of all knowledge claims. As the lively debates and developments in our period suggests, current feminist theory is not uniform or static, but rather a diverse array of voices and positions within distinct disciplinary and cultural settings. From the theoretical and epistemological analyses of racism and ethnocentricism, through the various debates on queer bodies and the gendered, relational human, to the critical appraisals of decolonization and value-free scientific technologies, feminist texts have challenged traditional methodologies for their radical disjunction, dichotomization, hierarchical arrangement, faulty universalization, and effacement of important qualifications.[20]

Among current feminist critiques, the ones that are most helpful to my current discussion are specific theoretical endeavors that address the displacement of rationalist discourses from any privileged relation to truth and knowledge. These analyses have unmasked the naïve notion of progress through reason, arguing that rationality has been construed as a male principle, and an undue emphasis placed on it has relegated women and other groups to secondary positions throughout the history of Western civilization. For many feminist philosophers, efforts to construct alternative models of knowledge are paramount to their existence within their disciplines. They point to the assumptions of Anglo-American philosophy, which tend to exclude women from the practice of philosophy because science has become the standard of rationality for it.

Feminist epistemologists, in particular, have addressed flawed conceptions of knowledge and objectivity, suggesting that dominant conceptions and practices of knowledge acquisition and justification have systematically disadvantaged women and other subordinated groups. They have also argued that science often affirms the unique contributions to culture made by transhistorical egos that reflect a reality only of abstract entities. Scientific veracity, they argue, has been substantiated by the administrative mode of interacting with nature and other inquirers; by impersonal and universal forms of communication; and by an ethic of socially autonomous—that is, value-free—pieces of evidence.[21] Here one recognizes intimations of the long-reaching effects of the Cartesian legacy in the subject versus object differentiation of scientific investigation and the individual versus society differentiation of political thought, leading to the now familiar conception of the world in terms of man/woman, culture/nature, rational/irrational, mind/body, public/private, and so on.

Within contemporary religious and theological feminism, Rosemary Ruether's work has most consistently and effectively addressed the conceptual and cultural effects of this Western dualism, initiating provocative discussions about nature, subjectivity, and knowledge.[22] Ruether has offered a feminist critique of patriarchal histories and scholarship that has included women's absence from the long history of post-Renaissance science and social theory, which has posited "man" as its object, either excluding women as unworthy of attention or, more recently, claiming to speak for women as well as men in an allegedly ungendered humanism. The aspect of Ruether's work that I think reverberates (however faintly) with the ethical force of Conway's religious naturalism is the feminist-inflected concept of ecojustice. In her distinctive style, Ruether has shown that the characteristic logical structure of dualism in dominant Euro-American philosophic-theological traditions is based on an alienated form of differentiation, a denial of dependency, and a representation of otherness, which has resulted in a monolithic view of nature. This dimension of Ruether's work also corroborates a fundamental religious conviction that I hold, namely, that humans are value-laden evolution made aware of itself, perfecting and creating love and goodness—or participating in world-formation—in enacting our radical relationality.

OVERVIEW OF ROSEMARY RUETHER'S ECOFEMINISM

Ruether was one of the first contemporary feminist religious scholars to perceive and articulate the interconnections between two seemingly disparate issues: the domination of nature and the domination of women (and humans more generally). Since at least 1971, she has argued for a religious and social vision that addresses both ecological degradation and social injustice:

> Women must see that there can be no liberation for them and no solution to the ecological crisis within a society whose fundamental model of relationships continues to be one of domination. They must unite the demands of the women's movements with those of the ecological movement to envision a radical reshaping of the basic socioeconomic relations and the underlying values of society.[23]

Ruether has ceaselessly reinterpreted the entire structure of basic Christian doctrines in light of modernity's obsession with the dread of death and the construction of human identity as outside nature. Her feminist trajectory has traced and assessed a male ideology of transcendent idealism, which involves seeing reality in terms of a whole chain of dualistic relations—male/female, soul/body, sprit/matter, culture/nature, in which the second half of each pair is seen as alien and subject to the first.[24] This logic of dualism has resulted in an instrumentalist treatment of nature, and has justified its exclusion from ethical significance in Western culture—an important insight that was conceived by Conway in the seventeenth century. In *To Change the World* (1981), Ruether insisted that the ecological crisis could not be resolved by merely adopting either a new personal ethic and worldview of symbiosis or a facile aesthetical appreciation of nature:

> An ecologic ethic cannot stop at protection of parks and rivers for wilderness hiking and camping for the leisure classes. We must recognize the hidden message of social domination that lies within the theological and ideological traditions of domination of nature. Man's domination of nature has never meant humans in general, but ruling class males. The hidden link in their domination of nature has always been the dominated bodies, the dominated labor of women, slaves, peasants, and workers.[25]

With other nonreligious ecofeminists, Ruether has further unmasked the mechanistic constructions of scientific discourse, arguing that solutions to global problems will not be found if contemporary citizens ignore the interconnectedness of all life—humans, and the creatures and plants with whom humans share the earth. They all suggest that the present task of liberating nature in all its myriad forms involves intelligent, unflinching critiques of the intersections of racism, classism, ageism, ethnocentricism, imperialism, colonialism, heterosexism, and sexism.[26]

I consider Ruether's nature-based feminism a crucial and important stage in the ongoing dissolution of modern constructions of compartmentalized, instrumentalized nature that Conway's critique of Descartes anticipated. In its desire to grasp the fullness and uniqueness of natural life, Ruether's ecotheological discourse reverberates with important values that emanate from Conway's early modern religious naturalism. In a recent work, *Gaia and God: An Ecofeminist Theology of Earth Healing*, she explores the construction of human consciousness, which invites further reflection on an eco-ethics of communal care. For

Ruether, human consciousness is the most intense and complex form of the inwardness of material energy itself as it bursts forth at that evolutionary level where matter is organized in the most complex and intensive way—the central nervous system and the cortex of the human brain.[27] Additionally, while we humans are unique in possessing our degree of self-consciousness, we also have much in common with non-human forms of life, and must therefore respond to a thou-ness in all beings. This experience of conversion—of recognizing that the special, intense form of radical energy of matter is not without continuity with other forms of life—requires humans learning how to convert intelligence into an instrument that can cultivate the harmonies and balances of an ecological community. According to Ruether, human consciousness is, and must be, where we recognize our kinship with all other beings: "The dancing void from which the tiniest energy events of atomic structures flicker in and out of existence and self-aware thought are kin along a continuum of organized life-energy."[28]

Such wisdom resonates astonishingly with Conway's vitalistic discourse and theory of monads in *The Principles*. Furthermore, Ruether's reenvisioned self conjures up Conway's early modern idiom of nature's interior movement supremely exemplified in human nature's movement toward the divine—and, in varying degrees, both thinkers point toward an important conviction that I hold, namely, that what humans do about their ecology depends on what they think about themselves in relation to other natural processes around them. In short, I think that human ecology is deeply conditioned by beliefs about nature and destiny—that is, by religion.

In the twentieth-first century, I invite religious humanists and naturalists to probe further into an important question posed by Ruether and others: What does it mean to be human nature interacting with other forms of nature? Within her ecojustice discourse, Ruether indicates that human awareness, or our self-reflective consciousness, is not a separable ontological substance, but rather an experience of our own interiority that is integral to our brain-body and dies with it. Her insight inspires one brave response, among many, which is the religious one of living humbly, yet joyously, in the immediacy of each moment and forfeiting a classic modernist strategy (described elsewhere by Mark C. Taylor as the ingenious unhappy conscious of modern subjectivity trying to master its self through a defiance of death).[29] Such a response involves a huge responsibility of reflection and action. Embracing our finitude—fully and passionately—leads to a renewed appreciation of human integrity in its interactions with other forms of nature.

As a Christian thinker, Ruether's investigations have often led her to radical religious reconstructions, as is evident in her conception of the symbol of divinity as the God/ess who is primal matrix, the ground of being—new-being—who is neither stifling immanence nor rootless transcendence.[30] While such reconstructive theism is appealing to some, it is not an essential category of analysis I find useful in advancing my own ecohumanist religious discourse. Nor am I persuaded that a call for theological reimaging through ecofeminist principles alone will persuade Western Christian citizens and their allies to go beyond introspective or privatized musings to communal environmental ethics and practices.

I am much more inspired by Ruether's equally provocative suggestion that Westerners also reexamine our notions of human subjectivity. I am very interested in asking how alternative conceptions of the human may increase the critical and analytical force of ethical values inherent in an ecological worldview, and in discerning its connection to cooperative political practices for liberation movements. Put more succinctly, I seek interpretive interventions or strategies that scrutinize and resist the dominant discursive formations (i.e., those particular configurations linking language and epistemology) on nature in its myriad forms, which are effectively gaining mastery of the world.

Distinct in its exaltation of demanding nature's liberation, my religious naturalism functions within the postmodern landscape to help recover the representations and articulations of alternate voices in philosophical, political, scientific, and poetic exchanges because the question of what can be said, when, and by whom, is of crucial significance. I thus propose a critical religious naturalism, or a certain sustained set of religious reflections on humans as natural organisms—in other words, I propose to conceive humans as evolution that has become aware of itself. This is a period in which the knowledge that humans are indeed an intrinsic, distinct part of evolution is pressing upon us with new force and urgency. The evolutionary past is indicative for us; it is also for us an imperative, in that it sets parameters that must be satisfied if we are to exist. At this juncture, then, one may speak of *homo sapiens* as the future of a seventeen billion past that is the universe—or, at least one of the futures. Future possibilities depend, in large part, on humans having a clear awareness of, and acting properly in accord with, this self-knowledge. Minimally, this means acknowledging that the symbolic language of science, in particular evolutionary biology, provides one (not the only) rich conceptual space for religious naturalists to further reflect on future possibilities and on human actualization.

Some religious scholars may question my suggestion, arguing that science, as the paradigmatic voice of twentieth-century academic disciplines, has maintained a self-serving, often misleading, pretense of dispassionate objectivity. Such critical posturing has helped promoted a dominant view of reality in which there is a sense of separation between self and other, between observer and observed, and between the active human knower and the passive object of inquiry. Others might insist that biological science still remains devoted to limited and problematic patriarchal conceptions, especially in its major depictions of evolutionary nature. Indeed, many Westerners have come of age in an intellectual environment in which evolution theory is taken for granted, and opposition to it is often identified with the regressive parochialism of religious fundamentalists. For most contemporary Westerners, evolution theory and the mechanisms of natural selection are the best available responses for crucial questions pertaining to life. Among these are: How did the current assortment of living forms come into existence? What explains the close fit between the characteristics of living beings and the environments they inhabit (i.e., the phenomenon of adaption)"?

These questions and responses, of course, evoke the figure of Darwin, a beneficiary of British imperialism, who spent five years of exploration as a naturalist aboard the *Beagle*. Among his many concerns, Darwin was interested to discover how the environment might act such that it could produce adaptive characteristics in successive generations of plants or animals. He sought clearer understandings of such processes as variation, population pressure, differential adaptedness, differential survival, and differential reproduction in biological life. Darwin chose the term "natural selection" to describe how slight variations in species survive, thereby producing new breeds of plants and animals, and in order to "mark its relation to [man's] power of selection."[31] Darwin saw in the course of adaptation and in the engine of evolutionary progress a fascinating principle: in the course of a competition, those best suited to an environment would be able to produce relatively more offspring; and that, by inheritance, their characteristics would predominate in the next generation. According to this principle, the purported randomness and confusion of the reproductive process are not significant since competition ensures a logic to its end product by the elimination of unfit parents before they could reproduce, or the survival of a relatively small number of their less fit offspring. One consequence of these principles is of a vision of the human situation based on putative laws of nature—or one could project on all of nature this fundamental principle.[32]

In its own historical growth as a compelling scientific notion, the theory of evolution has been intimately associated with dominant images of nature as a battleground and of life as essentially a competitive struggle with a limited number of places at the top. As various feminists have pointed out, social and economic variables aided in making evolutionary theory the Western world's most triumphant modern myth, or narrative. Darwin read economist and demographer Thomas Malthus's *Essay on the Principle of Population* (1798), whose culturally inflected notions of competition and scarcity were instrumental in Darwin's development of evolution.[33]

Challenging the optimistic belief of his contemporaries that population growth automatically generated more prosperity, Malthus suggested that since the number of people grew much faster than the amount of food, problems would inevitably arise. If one assumed scarcity of resources, especially food, a competition would ensue affecting the composition of successive generations. Consequently, Darwin expanded the idea of a general organic struggle for existence in which those members of a species that possessed traits favorable to survival in their particular circumstances would be most likely to reach reproductive age and hence would spread those traits through subsequent generations, thereby gradually changing the character of the population. Malthus's vision, however, was much more problematic when taken as social policy. He applied his principle of population to argue against the notion of human perfectibility, and critiqued the ethical impetus of the English "poor laws," which aimed in improving the lot of the economically disadvantaged. Such generosity, Malthus asserted, allowed the unfit—equated with the poor—to reproduce faster than the upper classes, who showed moral restraint. Malthus predicted that as a consequence humanity would deteriorate, and, unfortunately, his social theory conjures up nifty rationalizations of eugenics, of the culture of poverty, and of forced sterilization.[34]

In a complete reversal of Malthus's social vision, Edmund Spencer argued that higher biological organisms and more advanced societies showed the same features (greater differentiation, specialization, and individuation), and that both were composed of necessary functionary members whose division of labor allowed the mechanism to function. In the Spencerian schema, the theory of evolution becomes synonymous with progress and development from the simple to the more complex, organized whole. Spencer asserted, "The poverty of the inescapable, the distresses that come upon the imprudent, the starvation of the idle, and those shoulderings aside of the weak by the strong, which leave so many in shallows and in miseries, are the decrees of a large, far-seeing benevolence."[35] With his belief in the Lamarckian inheritance of functionally acquired traits present in the evolutionary process, Spencer believed the struggle for existence and the ensuing suffering were positive, helping to popularize the now famous notion, survival of the fittest.

Another problematic dimension of the modern evolutionary narrative, as several philosophers and historians of science have argued, is the manner in which it became a gender-inflected marker of early modern industrial capitalism, expressing patriarchal concerns with the problem of disorder in the reproductive process and preoccupation with its control.[36] Set within the cultural productions of nineteenth-century thought, theories of evolution and natural selection coincided with dominant cultural misogyny, symbolizing males' anxiety about women. Such anxiety was clearly displayed in the (male) medical establishment's preoccupation with women's (pathological) reproductive physiology, with their (uncontrolled) sexuality, and with their (hysterical) psychology. As men were engaging in political struggles with women, so, in the realm of evolutionary thought, male thinkers installed competition as the force that imposed order on the chaos they perceived in the processes of reproduction, which they associated with women. As a Foulcadian-inspired reading would suggest, it is more than a coincidence that the nineteenth-century medicalization of women's reproductive capacities—attempts to control and contain women's fecundity—paralleled the emphasis upon domination and competition in nature.[37] Today, apart from patriarchal interference, medical knowledge supports the fact that reproduction is a very orderly process. As these examples help reveal, evolutionary theory has become one of the West's most triumphant modern myths. Its episodes and events express the familiar sorts of processes and characteristics that modern humans (embodying a masculinist spirit) associate with promoting progress and creating a specific history characterized by competition, struggle, domination, hierarchy, and, even cooperation, if seen as a competitive strategy. As Mary Midgley wisely observes,

> The theory of evolution is not just an inert piece of theoretical science. It is, and cannot help being, also a powerful folktale about human origins. . . . Facts will never appear to us as brute and meaningless; they will always organize themselves into some sort of story, some drama. These dramas can indeed be dangerous. They can distort our theories, and they have distorted the theory of evolution perhaps more than any other. The only way in which we can control this kind of distortion is to bring the dramas

themselves out into the open, to give them our full attention, understand them better and see what part, if any, each of them ought to play both in theory and in life.[38]

ECOHUMANIST NATURALISM

Within the last twenty years, a revolutionary spirit among humanists, historians, and philosophers of science has shown the damaging and limiting effects of the dominant scientific worldview characterized by absolutism, authoritarianism, determinism, and androcentricism. Further, post-Kuhnian studies of science have presented challenges to what Sandra Harding calls the internalist epistemology, namely, a model that conceives science as successfully manipulating the world and discovering its laws because it is rooted in theory-free observation, in value-free knowing, and in unprejudiced modes of forming and testing hypotheses.[39] Harding goes further to suggest that a better model is that of constrained constructivism, or emphasizing how systematic knowledge-seeking is always just one factor in any culture, society, or social formation, shifting and transforming other elements—educational systems, legal systems, economic relations, religious beliefs and practices, state projects (such as war-making), gender relations—as it, in turn, is transformed by them. These developments compel some of us to move beyond sterile, fossilized views of natural life to imagine new possibilities.

One avenue toward that end, at least for me, is in following Conway's lead in integrating insights from Western science and religion as one engages in processes of world-formation. The subtlety of evoking Conway's image is not in reclaiming a naive vitalism, but rather in showing that we do not have to abandon religious valuing or marginalized traditions and knowledge bases in any attempt to create fuller visions of human nature and its role in ongoing life. In this era of interdisciplinary tensions and competing values, religious scholars, with other voices of the countertradition, are challenged to resist the dominant trajectory of scientism that informs our constructions of nature. We might, then, seek out possible alliances among specific forms of scientific, religious, and feminist valuing as we seek to modify dominant conceptualizations of human processes and non-human ones. The alliance, however, is not without its risks. Most Westerners are simultaneously dazzled by the incredible lifesaving and life-improving accomplishments of science (as in its direct application in technology) and intimidated by its life-threatening and life-killing technological achievements. Additionally, nonscientists are often mystified by its esoteric language and techniques. However, as Conway's example would remind us, continued retreat into dangerous isolationism is not an option—there is a need to gain access to the practices and to have familiarity with various conceptual languages, methods, and theories.

The diverse theories emerging from the current science and religion paradigm provide rich imagery and solid support for my articulations of a transformative religious naturalism. For instance, neurologists have emphasized the social character of cognition in animals and humans, providing various types of evidence for understanding humanity as symbol makers, creators of a world imbued with value, and as social organisms. For example, In *The Humanizing Brain*, Carol Albright and James Ashbrooke use Paul MacLean's notion of the tripartite brain to argue that the limbic system, which we share with other mammals, is the center of emotions that mobilize action and makes possible richer forms of relationship that involve empathy and caring for the young.[40] These factors, in turn, lead us to recognize emotion, social relationships, and other values often associated with traditional religious symbols as constitutive of human reality. The two also theorize about the role of the neocortex, as it is developed in primates and humans, as the center of interpretation, organization, and symbolic representation and rationality.

While some critics of MacLean have argued that the relationships between the three regions of the brain are more complex than he recognized, they acknowledge that a distinction of three functions of the brain might still lead to some of the assumptions outlined by Ashbrooke and Albright. Other neurologists maintain that even though humans seek meaning by viewing their lives in a cosmic and religious framework that is itself a human symbolic construct, the brain is part of the cosmos and a product of the cosmos. Its structures reflect the nature of the cosmos and whatever ordering and meaning-giving forces are expressed in its history.

Evolutionary biologists, sociobiologists, evolutionary psychologists, and philosophers are currently debating the extent to which one can argue that humans are value-driven decision systems with primary values built into us. Some of these theories suggest that one component of being human is the heightened awareness of our ability to make decisions self-consciously, to act upon those decisions, and to take responsibility for them.[41] Moreover, various biologists assert that evolutionary history shows a directionality, or a trend toward greater complexity and consciousness. They note an increase in the genetic information in DNA, and a steady advance in the ability of organisms to gather and process information about the environment and to respond to it.

Ursula Goodenough, for example, argues persuasively for a view of evolutionary theory that celebrates such directionality. For Goodenough, "life is getting something to happen against the odds and remembering how to do it. That something that happens is biochemistry and biophysics, the odds are beat by intricate concatenations of shape fits and shape changes, and the memory is encoded in genes and their promoters."[42] Using the metaphor of music as a bridge for understanding the complexities of evolution, Goodenough asserts that a good musicologist can often detect older forms or variations (a fugal texture, a specific cadence, or even a melodic strain) in new compositions. The music analogy helps her to describe the complexity of evolutionary life, too, as a fascinating organic composition of intricate movements where the old is woven with the new to generate something more. She states,

> A good biochemical idea—a protein domain that binds well to a promoter, a channel that's just the right size for a calcium ion—gets carried along through time, tweaked and modulated to best serve the needs of the current composition/organism but recognizable through evolutionary history. These conserved ideas combine with novelty to generate new direction, new ways of negotiating new environmental circumstances.[43]

Others agree that the human self emerges in a biological process that is affected by genes, but also by many other factors at higher levels. In human development, as in evolutionary history, selfhood is always social, a product of language, of culture, and of interpersonal interaction and genetic expression. These factors have led Ian Barbour, a major representative of the religion and science dialogue, to argue persuasively for a construction of the human individual as a multilevel psychosomatic unity that is both a biological organism and a responsible self.[44] Relying on the insights of neuroscience, computer science, and Western religion, Barbour advances a conception of the human as necessarily connected with such themes as embodiment, emotions, the social self, and consciousness. For Barbour, the notion of the human involves the integration of body and mind, reason and emotion, individual and social groups. He relies on the theoretical frameworks of neuroscientists who highlight these same features, including Michael Arbib's action-oriented schema theory, Joseph

LeDoux's study of emotions, and Leslie Brothers' analysis of the neural bases of social interaction.[45]

These ideas emerging from the scientific sphere are not so much prescriptive as they are suggestive in helping me propose an artful construction of humans as value-laden, social organisms in constant search of meaning (cognition), enamored of value (beauty), and instilled with a sense of purpose (telos). The human species, in my estimation, entails a modality of existence within a sphere of values in which transformation occurs. In short, I propose a view of humanity as pulsating organisms full of possibilities, desirous of novelty, and aimed toward transformation—all qualities associated with human valuation. As Konstantin Kolenda has suggested, the religious concept of God, or of any absolute value, has functioned as humanity's recognition of our longing to take our highest ideals or values seriously.[46] The very presence of this longing attests to the reality of religiousness, or of what I wish to call the religious impulse within humans. This experience of religiousness suggests a "divinizing" element to the construction of the humanity when one interprets the sacred as having an awareness or sense of distance between what we humans are and what we wish to be, or between the world as it is currently experienced and as it could be experienced. I believe that through it we might do as the poet Emily Dickinson beautifully encouraged us to— "dwell in possibility/a fairer house than prose."[47]

This religious impulse, irreducibly connected to the pulsating human organism, points to a tenacious refusal of humans to reduce our various actions to mere brute existence (or rather determinist forces and mechanistic explanations of cause/effect). I also associate this impulse with humans' ability to reflect upon the past, to assess the present, and, inevitably, to enact a future. In short, the religious impulse symbolically represents what the human organism or group might do with its concept of time, as a guide to behavior. Here I invoke Whitehead's view of religion as "the vision of something which stands beyond, behind, and within, the passing flux of immediate things; something which is real, and yet waiting to be realized; something which is a remote possibility, and yet the greatest of present facts . . . something that gives meaning to all that passes, and yet eludes apprehension."[48] This religious quality has been variously expressed as the desire to experience a profound intimacy with others, or perhaps to construct "worlds" of meaningful relations, or, sometimes, to discover fuller dimensions of reality beyond what appears obvious. Of course, the question of whether there may not be the possibility of something "more" or some positivity (however that is conceived) beyond what we currently experience has been (and continues to be) a persistently religious one.

One benefit of proposing the concept of humans as valuing, social organisms is that it may help dispel the illusion of the autonomous, atomistic self, thereby irrevocably negating much of what has been believed to be distinctively and normatively human in modernity. In the Western context, the ontotheological tradition, with its deity boasting of its aseity, has often and primarily esteemed the (male) subject as "the solitary self, whose self-consciousness assumes the form of an individual 'I' that defines itself by opposition to and transcendence of other isolated subjects."[49] Contrary to these assumptions, the conception of the valuing, relational human demonstrates a decentering of subjectivity that results in the loss of a static substance of center—once thought to be the basis of unique individuality. There is no isolated self who stands over against fields of interaction. There is no private self or final line between interiority and exteriority—we always include the other: "To the extent that the divinized human is a trace and subjectivity is tracing, the self is *primordially* relational and inevitably entangled in temporal becoming."[50] This conception of humanity also rejects the teleological task of humans reaching perfectibility, where perfectibility is the nullification of phenomenological and historical content—and thus of true historicity. A fuller sense of this pulsating, valuing human organism lies in our envisioning newer forms of embodied relationality that allow a vital flourishing among all sentient, natural entities. It involves human engagement with diverse processes of life.

VITAL FORCES OF LOVE

Those of us interested in advancing the concept of vital love as a human ideal (or an ennobling value, if you will) must take note of the plurality of perspectives that help to shape humans as valuing, social organisms. As I conceive it, this construction of humanity has a pivotal role to play in liberating and transforming all of nature, a task that is reminiscent of the symbolic power of Ruether's ecojustice discourse. I encourage religious humanists and our allies and friends—indeed, all who would listen—to continue creating and participating in various fields of feminist inquiry and activism, and to see without hesitation the interconnectedness of such issues as peace, labor, women's health care, antinuclear activity, the environment, and animal liberation. Expressed in the idiom of Goodenough, these cultural endeavors reveal our awareness of the interrelatedness of all creatures on the planet today. She reminds us that "Most of [my] genes are like gorilla genes, but they're also like many of the genes in a mushroom. [I] have more genes than a mushroom, to be sure, and some critical genes are certainly different, but the important piece to take in here is our deep interrelatedness, our deep genetic homology, with the rest of the living world."[51]

The notion of humanity as evolution aware of itself, as pulsating, communal value-laden organisms, points to locating selfhood and its experiences in concrete social relations, and not only in fictive or purely textual conventions. Here I stress the central importance of sustained, intimate relations with other processes and entities, and of the implications of such relations to the constitution, structure, and ongoing experiences of a self. Each self is partially constituted in and through networks of relations, fantasies, and expectations among and about external objects. This concept of the human self is also differentiated, local, and historical, echoing the challenges of distinct human natures whose historicities have often been left out of essentialist, grand social theories: the poor and working class, lesbians, physically challenged individuals, women and men of color, older women, queer identities. In other words, ideas about the valuing, social human are dependent on and made plausible by the existence of specific set of social relations, including gender, race, sexuality, and race in specific contexts.

With other feminist theorists, I also question the coherency of any emancipatory discourse without some implicit notion of an intentional human self. I think humans are most capable of being moral selves when we see ourselves as deeply connected with others, not just in our actions but also in our very constitution. We come to be by virtue of our relatedness, and so, too, we act (have agency) in relations with others. Furthermore, valuing, social humans may envision different practices, of expanded configurations of relationality, of new worlds—holding up a historicizing mirror to any given societal formation that compels a recognition of its transitory and fallible nature, such that more people realize that "what is" can be disassembled and improved.

Furthermore, my feminist consciousness argues that if we wish to avoid the ever-present dangers of modernism's illusions, we must write in various perspectives, modalities, and voices that have been pushed to the rear, so that we can enact critical standpoints by which to judge the present truths of the 'naturalized' world, particularly when they pretend to be the whole and only truth. In so doing, we help to bring to the fore forgotten traditions on myriad, processional nature that found expression in Conway, van Helmont, Driesch, Bergson, the Romantic poets and visionaries, Whitehead, Wieman, Ruether, and many others. Standing among the various strands of countertraditions operating in the postmodern era, religious naturalists might then begin postulating ethical theories that provide as fully as possible inclusive and global analyses of intersectional oppressions, insisting that ethical solutions to global problems will not be found if contemporaries ignore the interconnectedness of all life. The result may be a type of planetary ethics—as coined by Goodenough—where the vital forces of love, or of *élan vital*, promote an understanding of, and commitment to, the importance of valuing and preserving ecosystems (whether understood as organisms, individuals, populations, communities, and their interactions). Rather than seeing evolution as the metanarrative of an increasing capacity to manipulate other nature, or the progressive development of increased specialization, we now emphasize the successive emergence of new forms of opportunity, or the continual diversification of new modes of being, or new patterns of harmonious coexistence among nature.

Conway's historical example inspires us in these movements. Her early modern idiom was a crucial link in a trajectory of thought on nature that has yet to be fully explored for its power to provide new forms of relationality among diverse natural processes. Conway lived during an exciting time in which science, religion, and philosophy were inextricably intertwined, as is ours today. Hence, her presence looms above current attempts to assess, even celebrate, the fullness (the "more") of life as we reflect on processional nature, seeking transformations of self, of other, and of the world in which expressions of homophobia, sexism, racism, imperialism, and all of the other ideological dualisms that deny our radical and mutual relatedness are eradicated. I venture to say that these current movements are constitutive of the divine—humans conceiving and promoting activity among the complex, infinite richness of processional nature as we participate in goodness.

Notes

CHAPTER 1

1. Anne Conway, *The Principles of the Most Ancient and Modern Philosophy*, trans. and ed. Allison P. Coudert and Taylor Corse (Cambridge: Cambridge University Press, 1996). In 1690, a Latin translation of Conway's philosophical treatise, originally written in English by Conway, was published posthumously as *Principia philosophiae antiquissimae et recentissimae de Deo, Christos et creatura, id est de spiritu et material in genere* (Amsterdam, 1690). This Latin version of Conway's text was translated into English and published as *The Principles of the Most Ancient and Modern Philosophy Concerning God, Christ, and the Creatures* (Amsterdam, 1690; reprinted London, 1692).

2. Gilbert R. Owen, "The Famous Case of Lady Anne Conway," *Annals of Medical History* 9 (1937): 567–71.

3. See, for example, Charles Coulston Gillispie, *Genesis and Geology: A Study in the Relations of Scientific Thought, Natural Theology, and Social Opinion in Great Britain, 1760–1850* (Cambridge: Harvard University Press, 1951); Martin Rudwick, "Senses of the Natural World and Senses of God: Another Look at the Historical Relation of Science and Religion," in *The Sciences and Theology in the Twentieth Century*, ed. A. R. Peacocke (South Bend: Notre Dame University Press: 1981), 241–61; David C. Lindberg and Ronald L. Numbers, "Beyond War and Peace: A Reappraisal of the Encounter between Christianity and Science," *Church History* 55, no. 3 (September 1986): 338–54; David C. Lindberg and Ronald L. Numbers, *God and Nature: Historical Essays on the Encounter Between Christianity and Science* (Berkeley: University of California Press, 1986); John Hedley Brooke, *Science and Religion: Some Historical Perspectives* (Cambridge: Cambridge University Press, 1991).

4. In this book, I treat only general aspects of Conway's life, devoting much more attention to Conway's central ideas and showing their importance to contemporary developments in religious naturalism. For historical information regarding Conway's life, I consulted Marjorie Hope Nicolson and Sarah Hutton, eds., *The Conway Letters: The Correspondence of Anne, Viscountess Conway, Henry More, and their Friends (1642–1684* (Oxford: Clarendon Press, 1992); hereafter cited as *Conway Letters*.

5. *Conway Letters*, 1. Conway's father became Speaker of the House of Commons; her half-brother, Heneage Finch, successively Lord Keeper and Lord Chancellor under Charles II, was appointed Earl of Nottingham in 1681; and her nephew, Daniel Finch, played a significant part in late Stuart politics.

6. Ibid., 5, 15.

7. Ibid., Letter #13, "Lord Conway to his daughter-in-law, Anne Conway," July 1, 1654, 29–30; other letters from Lord Conway to Anne Conway include #14, July 8, 1651, 31–32; #15, July 22, 1651, 33–34; #16, September 20, 1651, 34–36; see also #17, "Anne Conway to her father-in-law," October 2/9, 1651, 36–38.

8. Ibid., 310. For further information on van Helmont, see Allison Coudert, "A Quaker-Kabbalist Controversy: George Fox's Reaction to Francis Mercury van Helmont," *Journal of the Warburg and Courtauld Institutes*, XXXIX (1976): 171–89 and *The Impact of the Kabbalah in the Seventeenth Century: The Life and Thought of Francis van Helmont (1614–1698)* (Leiden: E. J. Brill, 1998); Stuart Brown, "F. M. van Helmont: His Philosophical Connections and the Reception of his later Cabbalistical Philosophy (1677–1699)" in *Studies in Seventeenth-Century European Philosophy*, ed. M. A. Stewart (New York: Oxford University Press, 1997).

9. Ibid.

10. Angeline Goreau, *The Whole Duty of A Woman: Female Writing in Seventeenth-Century England* (New York: Dial Press, 1985), 5; hereafter cited as *The Whole Duty*.

11. Lady Margaret Cavendish (1623–73) was a contemporary of Hobbes and a member of the Newcastle Circle. She was one of the first English women to publish a large body of literary work (as opposed to religious tracts) under her own name. Cavendish published two volumes of verse, *Poems and Fancies* (1653) and *Philosophical Fancies* (1653), in which she presented an imaginative type of Hobbesian and Epicurean atomism. She also wrote on natural philosophy, and her books were widely circulated in the two decades following 1650. For further reading, see *Margaret Cavendish: Observations Upon Experimental Philosophy*, ed. Eileen O'Neill (Cambridge: Cambridge University Press, 2001); Margaret Cavendish, *The Blazing World and Other Writings*, ed. Katie Lillie (New York: Penguin Putnam, 1994); *Paper Bodies: A Margaret Cavendish Reader*, ed. Sylvia Bowerbank and Sara Mendelson (Orchard Park, N.Y.: Broadview Press, 2000); John H. Kargon, *Atomism in England from Hariot to Newton* (Oxford: Clarendon Press, 1966); Sarah Hutton, "Anne Conway, Margaret Cavendish and Seventeenth-Century Scientific Thought," in *Women, Science and Medicine 1500–1700: Mothers and Sisters of the Royal Society*, ed. Lynette Hunter and Sarah Hutton (Thrupp, Stroud, Gloucestershire: Sutton Publishing Limited, 1997), 218–34.

12. Margaret Cavendish, Duchess of Newcastle, *Sociable Letters* (London: 1664), quoted in Goreau, *The Whole Duty*, 7.

13. Bathsua Makin, *An Essay to Revive the Antient Education of Gentlewomen in Religion, Manners, Arts and Tongues* (London: 1673), quoted in Goreau, *The Whole Duty*, 25.

14. Ibid.

15. A number of seventeenth-century European women published literary essays and polemic tracts that defended women's right to work in philosophy and science. For example, Mary Astell (1666–1731), who proposed a plan for a school for women modeled along convent lines, wrote *A Serious Proposal to the Ladies for the Advancement of Their True and Greatest Interest. By a Lover of her Sex* (London: R. Wilkin, 1694) and *Some Reflections upon Marriage* (London: 1706). Catherine Trotter Cockburn (1679–1749) began her varied career as a playwright, but her interests soon turned to philosophy. Cockburn's first published essay in 1702 defended Locke against charges that his radical epistemology was materialistic and irreligious. Another essay, *The Works of . . . Theological, Moral, Dramatic and Poetical* was published in 1751 in London. Another notable figure was Elizabeth of Bohemia, one of Descartes' staunchest defenders who also raised important questions about his dualistic philosophy. Descartes dedicated *Principles of Philosophy* (1644) to Elizabeth, declaring that she understood his theories much more than any individual he had encountered. Finally, Anna Maria van Schurman (1607–78) was one of the most renowned women scholars of Europe, variously referred to as the Tenth Muse and the Minerva of Holland. Schurman was fluent in all the classical languages as well as lesser known ones like Syriac and Chaldee, and was widely respected as a Latinist. She corresponded with many of the famous scholars of her day, including Descartes, who was a friend. Schurman even critiqued Descartes' philosophy on religious grounds shortly after his *Discourse on Method* was published; in 1641, she published a treatise advocating women's rights to a classical education that was originally written in Latin. In 1659, an English translation was published under the title *The Learned Maid; or, Whether a Maid May Be a Scholar. A Logic Exercise Written in Latin by that Incomparable Virgin Anna Maria van Schurman of Utrecht.*

16. Allison P. Coudert, *Leibniz and the Kabbalah* (Dordrecht: Kluwer, 1995) and *The Impact of Kabbalah in the Seventeenth Century: The Life and Thought of Francis Mercury van Helmont* (Leiden: Brill, 1997). In both texts, Coudert argues that Francis Mercury van Helmont was a direct influence on both Leibniz and Anne Conway. In one moving passage in the latter, Coudert describes Leibniz and Helmont drinking a cup of cappuccino and Leibniz wondering where the monads in the coffee would pass in its next incarnation.

17. Gottfried Wilhelm Leibniz, "Letter to Thomas Burnet" (1697), quoted in *The Conway Letters*, 456. In *The Death of Nature* (New York: HarperCollins, 1980) 257, Carolyn Merchant translates this passage as follows: "My philosophical views approach somewhat closely that of the late Countess of Conway, and hold a middle position between Plato and Democritus, because I hold that all things take place mechanically as Democritus and Descartes contend against the views of Henry More and his followers, and hold too, nevertheless, that everything takes place according to a living principle and according to final causes—all things full of life and consciousness, contrary to the views of the Atomists." The issue of Conway's direct influence on Leibniz remains a topic of debate among historians and scholars. For two differing perspectives, see Carolyn

Merchant, "The Vitalism of Anne Conway," *Journal of the History of Philosophy,* XVII (1979): 225–69, and Stuart Brown, "Leibniz and More's Cabbalistic Circle," in *Henry More (1614–1687): Tercentenary Studies,* ed. Sarah Hutton (Dordrecht: Kluwer, 1990), 77–95.

CHAPTER 2

1. *The Conway Letters: The Correspondence of Anne, Viscountess Conway, Henry More, and their Friends (1642–1684),* ed. Marjorie Hope Nicolson and Sarah Hutton (Oxford: Clarendon Press, 1992), 317–18; hereafter cited as *Conway Letters.* In her introduction to this 1992 revised edition, Sarah Hutton addresses the difficulty of dating many of More's letters because he was not always careful to mention the year, and that on the whole she has accepted the Nicolson datings. In the few cases where it is impossible to know definitely the actual date of certain letters, she has suggested different dates, placing conjectural dates in square brackets. In this study, I follow Hutton's editorial emendations and dating, and I also incorporate several new letters that she has added that were omitted in the 1930 edition, as found in Appendices B and C.

2. Ibid., *Appendix B, Add MSS,* #19*a,* "Henry More to Anne Finch," September 9, [1650], 484–85; #19*b,* "Henry More to Anne Conway," May 5, [1651], 486–89; "#24*a,* "Anne Conway to Henry More," December 3, 1651, 493–94.

3. Ibid., #242, "Henry More to Lady Conway," September 17, 1674, 392–93; #199*a,* "Henry More to Lady Conway," August 6, [1670], 511.

4. Ibid., #238, "Henry More to Lady Conway," February 23, 1673–74, 385.

5. Ibid., #242*a,* "Lady Conway to Sir George Rawdon," September 25, 1674, 534.

6. Barry Reay, *The Quakers and the English Revolution* (London: Temple Smith, 1985), 13–14. Although their critics often lumped these groups together, much theological diversity existed among them. The Seekers, for example, were not, strictly speaking, a sect, but rather dissatisfied people searching for truth either as free individuals or as participants in a simple structured fellowship of kindred spirits. The English Baptists were spiritual descendants of continental Anabaptists. The Socinians were followers of Faustus and Laelius Socinus, Italian Protestant theologians and forerunners of what would become known as Unitarianism. They accepted Christ as the Messiah but denied both his divinity and the doctrine of the Trinity. The Socinians also stressed the innate goodness and rationality of humanity. The Muggletonians were named for Ludwicke, an English tailor and visionary, who, with his cousin John Reeves, denied the Trinity and proclaimed a new spiritual and political dispensation resembling the kingdom of God. Their numbers were never large and some became Quakers. The Levelers called for a "practical Christianity," which took action against various forms of oppression, pressing for a radical decentralization of political power through democratic reform of parliament. The Ranters took the antinomian view that all things are pure to the Christian and that sin exists only in the imagination. They also became a political force

during the Restoration period. The Diggers, led by Gerrard Winstanley, advocated and practiced for a brief period a type of agrarian communism. Some of their beliefs made them the target of early Quaker scorn. For further study, see Christopher Hill, *The World Turned Upside Down: Radical Ideas During the English Revolution* (New York: Viking Press, 1972); Christopher Hill, *A Nation of Change and Novelty: Radical Politics, Religion, and Literature in Seventeenth-Century England* (New York: Routledge, 1990); John Ferguson, *Politics Quaker Style* (San Bernardino, Calif.: The Borgo Press, 1995); Rosemary Moore, *The Light in their Consciences: The Early Quakers in Britain 1646–1666* (University Park: Pennsylvania State University, 2000).

7. *Conway Letters*, #198a, "Henry More to Lady Conway," June 3, [1670], 503–6; #199a, "Henry More to Lady Conway," August 6, [1670], 506–11; #200, "Henry More to Lady Conway," September 15, 1670, 305–8; #211, "Henry More to Lady Conway," July 14, 1671, 339–43. Scholars have substantiated More's suspicions, showing direct connections between Familist and Quaker communities in seventeenth-century England. For further study, see Christopher Hill, *The World Turned Upside Down: Radical Ideas During the English Revolution* (New York: Viking Press, 1972); Margaret Spufford, *Contrasting Communities* (Cambridge: Cambridge University Press, 1974); Rufus M. Jones, *Studies in Mystical Religion* (London: Macmillan, 1909). For studies exploring the possible connections between Quaker theology and Hermeticism, see G. F. Nuttall, "Unity with the Creation: George Fox and the Hermetic Philosophy," *Friends Quarterly* 1 (1947): 137–43; Richard Bailey, *New Light on George Fox and Early Quakerism* (San Francisco: Mellen Research University Press, 1992).

8. Alistair Hamilton, *The Family of Love* (Cambridge: Cambridge University Press, 1981), 24–34. A small early sect known as the Family of the Mount shared many values with the Familists. About 1610, an obscure religious sect began at Grindleton, Yorkshire, exhibiting Familist leanings. Described as the Grindleton Familists, this group continued into the 1660s. Probably only numbering in the hundreds at their height in England, Familists were present at the Court of Elizabeth I, James I, and Charles I. Many appeared to be people of position and learning, valued for their opinions and loyalty to the Crown against persistent outcries from those of other religious persuasions, especially the Puritans. For further study, see Christopher Marsh, *The Family of Love in English Society, 1550–1630* (Cambridge: Cambridge University Press, 1994).

9. Christopher Marsh, *The Family of Love in English Society, 1550–1630* (Cambridge: Cambridge University Press, 1994), 17–22.

10. John Knewstub, *A Confutation of Monstrous and Horrible Heresies Taught by H. N.* (London: T. Dawson for R. Sergier, 1579), quoted by Rufus M. Jones, *Studies in Mystical Religion* (London: Macmillan, 1909), 443.

11. *Conway Letters*, #194, "Henry More to Mrs. Elizabeth Foxcroft," June 10, 1669, 297.

12. Ibid., #256, "Henry More to Lady Conway," January 10, 167[6], 418.

13. Ibid., #200, "Henry More to Lady Conway," September 15, 1670, 307.

14. Henry More, *The Easie, True, and Genuine Notion, and Consistent Explication of the Nature of a Spirit, Whereby the Possibility of the Existence of Spirits,*

Apparitions, and Witchcraft is Further Confirmed (London: J. Flescher, for W. Morton, [1671] [1689], 1966); *An Explanation of the Grand Mystery of Godliness; Or, A True and Faithful Representation of the Everlasting Gospel of our Lord and Saviour Jesus Christ, the Onely Begotten Son of God and Sovereign over Men and Angels* (London: J. Flesher, for W. Morton, 1660); *Enthusiasmus Triumphatus, Or, A Brief Discourse of the Nature, Causes, Kinds, and Cure, of Enthusiasm* [1662] in *A Collection of Several Philosophical Writings*, Vol. I (New York and London: Garland, 1978). See also Daniel Fouke, *The Enthusiastical Concerns of Dr. Henry More: Religious Meaning and the Psychology of Delusion* (Leiden: E. J. Brill, 1997).

15. *Conway Letters*, #256, "Henry More to Lady Conway," January 10, 167[6], 417–18.

16. Ibid., #257, "Lady Conway to Henry More," February 4, 167[6], 422.

17. Barry Reay, "Quakerism and Society," in *Radical Religion in the English Revolution*, ed. J. McGregor and B. Reay (London: Oxford University Press, 1984), 149–51; Barry Reay, *The Quakers and the English Revolution* (London: Temple Smith, 1985), 43, 98.

18. *Conway Letters*, #253, "Lady Conway to Henry More," November 29, 1675, 409.

19. Ibid., #254, "Henry More to Lady Conway," December 7, [1675], 414.

20. Ibid., #255, "Henry More to Lady Conway," December 29, 1675, 416.

21. Ibid., #251, "Henry More to Lady Conway," November 9, 1675, 404.

22. Ibid., #241, "Henry More to Lady Conway," August 11, 1674, 391–92.

23. Henry More, *An Explanation of the Grand Mystery of Godliness* (London: Flesher and Morden, 1660), Book I, Ch. 6, 14. See also *Conway Letters*, #255, "Henry More to Lady Conway," December 29, 1675, 415.

24. *Conway Letters*, #256, "Henry More to Lady Conway," January 10, 167[6], 419.

25. Ibid., #257, "Lady Conway to Henry More," February 4, 1675[6], 422.

26. Ibid., #260a, "Lord Conway to {Sir George Rawdon}" (Extract), June 23, 1676, 535.

27. Ibid., #250, "William Penn to Lady Conway," 20th 8 mo, 1675, 402–3.

28. Ibid., #253, "Lady Conway to Henry More," November 29, 1675, 407.

29. George Keith, *Immediate Revelation* (London: 1675), 230.

30. The Kabbalah is not a single system of thought but a diverse set of mystical writings evolving over eight centuries, and revealing individual writers and schools, as well as distinct stages of developments. In this study, I focus on the Lurianic Kabbalah, which is identified with the creative efforts of Isaac Luria (1534–72), because it is the tradition that Conway and her contemporaries read and studied. These investigations by Conway and others were part of a larger Christian Kabbalah movement, which became a part of European magical and scientific traditions when it was integrated with the wide realm of the "occult" in the work of Cornelius Agrippa of Nettesheim. The Kabbalah had a significant influence on the works of English scientists and magicians like John Dee, Francis Bacon, Robert Fludd, and Michael Maier in Germany. In France, Guillaume Postel, a mystic and visionary, translated various Kabbalah texts. Then, of course, there is the work of van Helmont and others, drawing

from the Lurianic Kabbalah. Contemporary scholars are just beginning to assess the profound influence the Lurianic Kabbalah had on such intellectual luminaries as Newton and Leibniz. Newton secretly studied the Kabbalah, finding ideas in it that bore striking resemblance to some of his greatest scientific discoveries. The Kabbalah also profoundly influenced Leibniz, perhaps as a result of his interactions with van Helmont.

31. Klaus Reichert, "Christian Kabbalah in the Seventeenth Century," in *The Christian Kabbalah: Jewish Mystical Books and their Christian Interpreters*, ed. Joseph Dan (Cambridge: Harvard College Library, 1997), 127–48. Reichart argues that the Christian Kabbalist movement was not a short-lived, irrelevant phenomenon that was washed away by broad stream of intellectual and scientific development. Rather, this development exerted its influence in various and vastly different disciplines, a fact that is still primarily unrecognized by many contemporary scholars.

32. Allison Coudert, *The Impact of the Kabbalah in the Seventeenth-Century: The Life and Thought of Francis Mercury van Helmont (1614–1698)* (Leiden: Brill 1998), 111; hereafter cited as *Impact of Kabbalah*. For further study, see Moshel Idel, *Hasidism: Between Ecstasy and Magic* (Albany: State University of New York Press, 1995); Gershom Scholem, *Major Trends in Jewish Mysticism* (New York: Schocken, 1974) and *Origins of the Kabbalah*, trans. R. J. Zwiwerblowski (Princeton: Princeton University Press, 1987); Moshel Idel, *Kabbalah: New Perspectives* (New Haven: Yale University Press, 1988); Peter Schefer, *The Hidden and Manifest God: Some Major Themes in Early Jewish Mysticism*, trans. Aubrey Pomerantz (Albany: State University of New York Press, 1992).

33. George Keith to Knorr von Rosenroth, January 1676, quoted and translated in Coudert, *Impact of Kabbalah*, 187.

34. Van Helmont and Keith wrote a collaborative project: *Two Hundred Queries Moderately Propounded Concerning the Doctrine of the Revolution of Humane Soules, and its Conformity to Christianity (1684)*; van Helmont also wrote *Cabbalistical Dialogue in Answer to the Opinion of a Learned Doctor in Philosophy and Theology (1682)*. Finally, of course, there is Conway's treatise, *The Principles of the Most Ancient and Modern Philosophy*. Allison Coudert argues that all three texts display a deep commitment to the Kabbalah, and that they show how much Conway, Keith, and van Helmont appropriated key concepts from the *Kabbalah denudata* (specifically, the section "Concerning the Revolution of Souls").

35. *Conway Letters*, #253, "Lady Conway to Henry More," November 29, 1674, 408.

36. Ibid., #255, "Henry More to Lady Conway," December 29, 1675, 416. More wrote: "What you say of G. K. embracing of the opinion of Jewe concerning plurality of soules in one body, he is so greedy after the conceit of being infallibly inspired, that he will swallow anything, that will nourish that in him."

37. Anne Conway, *The Principles of the Most Ancient and Modern Philosophy*, trans. and ed., Allison P. Coudert and Taylor Corse (Cambridge: Cambridge University Press, 1996), 38, 42–43, 35, 61.

38. Coudert, *Impact of the Kabbalah*, 145.

39. Sanford Drob, *Kabbalist Metaphors: Jewish Mystical Themes in Ancient and Modern Thought* (Northvale, N.J.: Jason Aronson, 2000), 27.

40. One of More's fullest statement of his kabbalistic explorations is found in *Conjectura Cabbalistica* (1653), in which he offered overlapping readings of the first Book of Genesis: literal, moral, and philosophical. Later in life, More encountered genuine kabbalistic texts, through the German scholar Christian Knorr von Rosenroth. Nicolson includes a letter from More to Conway in her collection, and she also mentions a letter to Knorr von Rosenroth dated 1675, which was printed in the *Kabbala denudata*, II, 175. See also Coudert, *Impact of the Kabbalah*, 233.

41. Coudert gives an detailed account of these developments, culminating in what Quaker historians call the "Keithian Controversy" as well as its aftermath—van Helmont's break with the Quakers and Keith's growing theological conservatism—in chapter eleven, "The Quakers Rejection of the Kabbalah," in *Impact of the Kabbalah*, 240–70.

42. *Conway Letters*, 534–35.

43. Robert Barclay to the Princess Elizabeth, *Reliquae Barclaianae* (London: 1870), 21–22, quoted in Coudert, *Impact of the Kabbalah*, 213.

44. Letter to Landgraf Ernst van Hessen-Rheinfels, AK, I, 3: 260, quoted in Coudert, *Impact of Kabbalah*, 213–14.

45. *Conway Letters*, #263, "Henry More to Lady Conway," April 3, 1677, 430.

46. Richard Ward, *The Life of the Learned and Pious Dr. Henry More* (Cambridge: 1710), 76.

47. W. K. Jordan, *The Development of Religious Tolerance in England, Vols. I–III* (Cambridge: Harvard University Press, 1932–38), Vol. III, 1776–77.

48. *Conway Letters*, 412–13.

49. Princess Elizabeth to Robert Barclay, *Reliquae Barclaianae*, 27, quoted in Coudert, *Impact of the Kabbalah*, 214.

50. *Conway Letters*, #257, "Lady Conway to Henry More," February 4, 167[6], 421–22.

51. Ibid., #273, "Lord Conway to his wife," October 30, 1678, 443–44.

52. Ibid., #277, "Lord Conway to his wife," January 8, 167[9], 446.

53. Ibid., #257, "Lady Conway to Henry More," February 4, 167[6], 421.

54. Reay, *Quakers and the English Revolution*, 12–14. Reay writes that by the time the Quakers had arrived on the scene at the beginning of 1650s, the nation had been through two civil wars. A king and his archbishop of Canterbury had been tried and executed. The House of Lords, the institution of bishops, church courts, the Star Chamber, and Court of High Commission had been abolished. The army had become a power broker, much in the way that it has in many third world nations today; legislative assemblies were to arrive and depart according to the wishes of the military.

55. Cromwell sincerely tried to secure toleration for all sects except the Catholics, and the army on the whole supported him in this, for the core of the "New Model" consisted of Independents and other sects who believed that the war against the king was waged for religious as well as political

liberty. This was the fundamental reason for their opposition to royalist An-
glicans as well as to covenanting Presbyterians, for the Anglican prelates and
nobles as well as the Presbyterian ministers were against religious tolerance of
any but the established religion.

56. Reay, *Radical Religion in the English Revolution*, 149–50. Before 1725,
Quakers had published over eighty religious confessions and journals. In the
second one hundred years of Quakerism, fewer Quakers were having burning
religious experiences, and the novel became a popular genre of writing, hence
lesser Quaker classics were produced.

57. Jean-Luc Nancy, "Corpus," in *Thinking Bodies*, ed. Juliet Flower
MacCannell and Laura Zakarin (Palo Alto: Stanford University Press, 1994), 21.

58. Ibid., 27.

59. Ibid., 26.

60. Ibid.

61. Hugh Barbour and Arthur Roberts, eds., *Early Quaker Writings 1650–
1700* (Grand Rapids, Mich.: Eerdmans, 1973), 145. Although George Fox is
viewed as the recognizable founder of the Religious Society of Friends (FRS),
early historical accounts show that the movement formed itself almost spon-
taneously as more and more people accepted the professions and practices of
George Fox, having discovered in them the means by which they could bring
their lives into closer accord with God. Many historical records also suggest
that Fox himself did not have any idea of "founding" a church. A church, to
his mind, was simply a group of people whose common purpose it was to
relate themselves in love to God and with each other. Such a group can begin
and grow and its members could develop characteristics sufficiently alike to
justify their being called by a like name. Early Quaker practices challenged the
status quo and made Quakers the target of civil leaders' distrust and persecution. What the Friends stood for threatened the authority of those in power
and would dismantle the existing social and political order, which was cor-
rupt along class, gender, and economic lines.

62. Hugh Barbour, *The Quakers in Puritan England*, with a foreword by
Roland Bainton (New Haven: Yale University Press, 1964). In this text, Barbour
shows the importance of Puritan theology in shaping the consciousness of
early Quakers. For his discussion on how ecclesiastical neglect and exploita-
tion also played an important role in the early stages of the movement, see 1–
32 and 72–93.

63. Robert Fouke, *The Enthusiastical Concerns of Dr. Henry More*, 136. See
also Rosemary Moore, *The Light in Their Consciences* (University Park: Penn
State University, 2000), 40–41.

64. Hugh Barbour and Arthur Roberts, *Early Quaker Writings*, 73–74.

65. Richard Bailey, *New Light on George Fox and Early Quakerism: The
Making and Unmaking of a God* (Lewiston, N.Y.: Mellen University Press, 1992),
19, 22.

66. George Fox, *The Journal of George Fox*, ed. N. Penney (Cambridge:
Cambridge University Press, 1925), 97. For Fox's perspectives on the potential
perfectibility of humanity, see 101. Beginning in the 1670s, as a result of the

writings of Barclay and Penn, Fox's radicalism is played down and attributed to a misunderstanding of his words by hostile critics. His work and ideas were suppressed in the interest of producing the respectable, humanitarian Quakerism we know today.

67. Patricia Crawford, *Women and Religion in England 1500–1720* (New York: Routledge, 1993), 197. Crawford argues that as the Quakers became more institutionalized and socially acceptable, and as later leaders systematized Quaker teachings, many of these early freedoms were forfeited.

68. Ibid., 34.

CHAPTER 3

1. Generally speaking, natural philosophers or "amateur scientists" of England eventually sought to make their studies free of normative involvement in religious or political issues. This clear demarcation of science and religion in the seventeenth century is far from evident when one studies the specific (and more positive) views of influential scientists of the day. For example, in *The History of the Royal Society* (1667), Thomas Sprat, a famous chemist, made explicit the images of nature as a temple and the scientist as priest. There were also many other figures in the late seventeenth century, Robert Boyle (1627–91) and John Ray (1627–1705) among them, who envisaged scientific inquiry as a form of worship.

2. Anthony Grafton, "The Availability of Ancient Works," in *The Cambridge History of Renaissance Philosophy*, ed. Charles B. Schmitt, Quentin Skinner, and Eckhard Kessler (Cambridge: Cambridge University Press, 1988), 767–91. The Renaissance recovery of classical texts made alternative ancient philosophies of nature available to humanistically oriented natural philosophers. Plato's dialogues, Lucretius' exposition of ancient atomism in *De rerum natura*, and the Hermetic corpus, all of which had been little known before the fifteenth century, were of particular significance to these thinkers.

3. Francis Bacon, *The New Organon* (*Novum Organum*), Vol. IV, in *The Works of Francis Bacon*, 14 Vols, ed. J. Spedding, R. L. Ellis, and D. D. Heath (London: 1857–1874), 254–55. In *The New Organon*, Bacon provided a full-scale and systematic methodology for the reform of knowledge, replacing the sterile sophistries of scholasticism with a new program of inductive and experiments. For further study, see Michael Hunter, *Science and Society in Restoration England* (Cambridge: Cambridge University Press, 1981), 14–15. According to Hunter, the devotion to careful observation and experiment that is often seen as most characteristically "Baconian" had more varied roots.

4. Joseph Glanville, *Scepsis Scientifica, or the Vanity of Dogmatizing,* ed. John Owen (London: 1885), 127.

5. Henry Power, *Experimental Philosophy, in Three Books: Containing New Experiments, Microscopal, Mercurial, Magnetical,* ed. M. B. Hall (London: 1664; reprint, New York: Johnson Reprint Corporation, 1966), 197–207.

6. For the Aristotelians, various natures exist that endow bodies with tendencies to move in characteristic ways. For example, heavy bodies, because of their nature, tend to move toward their place at the center of the world; or the nature of the oak tree, potentially contained in the acorn, causes the constituent matter to be formed into an oak tree, rather than a maple. Many Renaissance philosophers in the Neoplatonic, Hermetic, and Paracelsian traditions portrayed a highly animistic world, characterized by sympathies and antipathies, acting at a distance and endowing the material world with its own, innate activity. For further study, see Charles B. Schmitt, *Aristotle and the Renaissance* (Cambridge: Harvard University Press, 1983).

7. Rene Descartes, *Discourse on the Method of Rightly Conducting One's Reason and Seeking the Truth in the Sciences*, in *The Philosophical Works of Descartes*, trans. John Cottingham, Robert Stoothoff, and Dugald Murdoch (Cambridge: Cambridge University Press, 1985), 136 (subsequent citations from Descartes' works are from this edition, designated as either Vol. 1 or Vol. II).

8. Michael Hunter, *Science and Society in Restoration England* (Cambridge: Cambridge University Press, 1981), 162.

9. Thomas Hobbes, *Leviathan*, ed. and introd. Crawford Brough Macpherson (Harmondsworth: Penguin, 1968), 8, 108, 113, 171.

10. Bacon, *The New Organon*, II, ii, ix.

11. Stephen Gaukroger, John Schuster, and John Sutton, eds., *Descartes' System of Natural Philosophy* (New York: Routledge, 2000), 4.

12. *The World*, in Cottingham, *The Philosophical Works of Descartes*, Vol. I, 90.

13. Ibid., 91–93.

14. *Meditation on First Philosophy*, "Second Meditation" in Cottingham, *The Philosophical Works of Descartes*, Vol. II, 22.

15. Daniel Garber, "A Different Descartes: Descartes and the programme for a mathematical physics in his correspondence" in *Descartes' System of Natural Philosophy*, 113–30. On page 114, Garber cites Alexandre Koyre: "The fact is well-known. Descartes' physics, as presented in *The Principia*, contains no expressible mathematical laws. It is, in fact, as little mathematical as that of Aristotle." In his essay, Garber also offers another perspective, namely, that in Descartes' correspondence, particularly his correspondence with Mersenne, one finds a capable mathematical physicist.

16. *The Principles of Philosophy*, Part II, in Cottingham, *The Philosophical Works of Descartes*, Vol. I, 232–44.

17. *Meditations on First Philosophy*, "Second Meditation," in Cottingham, *The Philosophical Works of Descartes*, Vol. II, 17–18.

18. Robert H. Kargon, *Atomism in England from Hariot to Newton* (Oxford: Clarendon Press, 1966), 1–4. See also 63–76 for a discussion on the reception of Descartes' theory by atomists of the Newcastle Circle, a group that included Hobbes.

19. *Meditations on First Philosophy*, "Fourth Meditation," in Cottingham, *The Philosophical Works of Descartes*, Vol. II, 40.

20. Ibid., "Third Meditation," 28.

21. Ibid., "Fifth Meditation," 48.

22. Henry More, *Defence of the Threefold Cabbala*, in *A Collection of Several Philosophical Writings* (London: 1662), 104.

23. Ibid., 79.

24. Quoted in Joseph Levine, "Latitudinarians, Neoplatonists, and the Ancient Wisdom," in *Philosophy, Science, and Religion in England 1640–1700*, ed. Richard Kroll (Cambridge: Cambridge University Press, 1992), 97.

25. Henry More, *Democritus Platonissans* (1646), quoted in Alan Gabby, "Henry More and the Limits of Mechanism," in *Henry More (1614–1687): Tercentenary Studies*, ed. Sarah Hutton (Nordrecht: Kluwer, 1990), 20.

26. Carolyn Merchant, *The Death of Nature* (New York: Harper SanFrancisco, 1980), 243.

27. Anne Conway, *The Principles of the Most Ancient and Modern Philosophy*, ed. Allison P. Coudert and Taylor Corse (Cambridge: Cambridge University Press, 1996), 63–64; hereafter cited as *The Principles*.

28. Lesser-known vitalists were the anatomists William Harvey and Francis Glisson, whose investigations often led them into dangerous areas with respect to faith. Glisson was the Regius Professor of Medicine at Cambridge and a leading physician at the College of Physicians in the 1640s and 1650s. His efforts to secularize the notion of life, that is, proclaiming the living and perceptive nature of matter, or that nature was alive, were perceived as heretical by More and Cudworth, and duly criticized by them.

29. Several prominent themes in Conway's way's text reflect her appropriation of kabbalistic doctrines. For further information, see Coudert and Corse's introductory comments in their edition, xviii–xxii. Henry More studied kabbalistic literature and also researched such phenomena as witchcraft, spirits, ghosts, demons, and angels. For further study, see Richard Popkin, "The Spiritualistic Cosmologies of Henry More and Anne Conway," in *Henry More (1614–1687): Tercentenary Studies*, ed. Sarah Hutton (Dordrecht: Kluwer, 1990), 97–114.

30. Conway, *The Principles*, 24.

31. Ibid., 15.

32. Ibid., 23.

33. Ibid. In the text, there are explicit references to the *Kabbala denudata* I, Pt.: I, 28, 30; Pt. 2, 37 ff; Pt. 3, 31–64; II, Pt. 3, 244 and last tract, 6, 7–26.

34. Ibid, 44–45.

35. Ibid., 32, 45.

36. Ibid., 63.

37. Ibid., 41–42.

38. Ibid., 49.

39. Ibid., 66.

40. Ibid., 40.

41. "Concerning the Revolution of Souls," in *Kabbala denudata II* (1684), 3: 244–78, quoted in Allison Coudert, *The Impact of the Kabbalah in the Seventeenth-Century: The Life and Thought of Francis Mercury van Helmont (1614–1698)* (Leiden: Brill 1998), 122; hereafter cited as *Impact of Kabbalah*.

42. Lawrence Fine, *Physician of the Soul, Healer of the Cosmos: Isaac Luria and His Kabbalistic Fellowship* (Palo Alto: Stanford University Press, 2003), 128.

43. Quoted in Coudert, *Impact of Kabbalah*, 120. For further study, see Moshel Idel, *Hasidism: Between Ecstasy and Magic* (Albany: State University of New York Press, 1995); Gershom Scholem, *Major Trends in Jewish Mysticism* (New York: Schocken, 1941); Gershom Scholem, *Origins of the Kabbalah*, trans. R. J. Zwiwerblowski (Princeton: Princeton University Press, 1987); Moshe Idel, *Kabbalah: New Perspectives* (New Haven: Yale University Press, 1988); Peter Schefer, *The Hidden and Manifest God: Some Major Themes in Early Jewish Mysticism*, trans. Aubrey Pomerantz (Albany: State University of New York Press, 1992).

44. Sanford Drob, *Kabbalist Metaphors: Jewish Mystical Themes in Ancient and Modern Thought* (Northvale, N.J.: Jason Aronson, 2000), 11. Luria believed that in order for there to be a place for the world, God had to withdraw from a part of Godself. This doctrine of *tsimtsum* (withdrawal) both symbolized exile in the deepest sense, within the divinity itself, and it also implied that evil was intrinsic to the creation process and not attributable to humanity alone. Allison Coudert suggests that this emphasis on human perfecting itself is the aspect of Luria's work that most appealed to Knorr and van Helmont, and was later introduced to Conway. Knorr and van Helmont were eventually swayed by the doctrine of transmigration, believing it offered the surest foundation of a universal Christian church.

45. Conway, *The Principles*, 42.

46. Ibid., 46.

47. Ibid., 58.

48. See Descartes' letter to Elizabeth of October 6, 1645 in *Philosophical Letters*, trans. Anthony Kenny (Minneapolis: University of Minnesota Press, 1970), 178. See also Albert A. Johnstone, "The Bodily Nature of the Self or What Descartes Should Have Conceded Elizabeth of Bohemia," in *Giving the Body its Due*, ed. Maxine Sheets-Johnstone (Albany: State University of New York Press, 1992), 16–47. Descartes' *Principles of Philosophy* contained a dedication to Elizabeth, whom he deemed the one individual who understood his writings more thoroughly than anyone he had encountered.

49. Conway, *The Principles*, 45–46.

50. Ibid., 64.

51. Ibid., 66.

52. Ibid., 67.

53. Ibid., 66.

54. Ibid., 38–39.

55. Ibid., 69.

CHAPTER 4

1. Among the fundamental conceptual ideas establishing Enlightenment ideology was the notion of a coherent, unitary, or stable self; the optimistic and rationalist philosophy of human nature; a rationalistic and teleological

philosophy of history, and a distinctive political philosophy (the moral) that posits the complex and necessary interconnections between reason, autonomy, and freedom. For further discussion, see C. W. White, *Triangulating Positions: Poststructuralism, Feminism and Religion* (Amherst, N.Y.: Humanity Books, 2002), 4.

2. Theodore Roszak, *Where the Wasteland Ends: Politics and Transcendence in Postindustrial Society* (New York: Doubleday, 1972), 264.

3. Anne Conway, *The Principles of the Most Ancient and Modern Philosophy*, ed. Allison P. Coudert and Taylor Corse (Cambridge: Cambridge University Press, 1996), 47.

4. Aristotle, "Metaphysics," in *Readings in Ancient Greek Philosophy: From Thales to Aristotle*, ed. S. Marc Cohen, Patricia Curd, and C. D. C. Reeve (Indianapolis/Cambridge: Hackett, 2005), 797.

5. Charlotte Witt, *Ways of Being: Potentiality and Actuality in Aristotle's Metaphysics* (Ithaca: Cornell University Press, 2003), 11–13.

6. *The Metaphysics: Aristotle* (Great Books in Philosophy), trans. John H. McMahon (Amherst, N.Y.: Prometheus Books, 1991), 237; Wilhelm Windelband, *History of Philosophy* (New York: Macmillan, 1910), 146.

7. Galen, *On the Natural Faculties* [Computer File] trans. Arthur John Brock (Seattle, Wash.: Electronic Scholarly Publishing Project, 2001), Book III, see esp. Sections 14 and 15; available from http://www.esp.org/books/galen/natural-faculties/html; Internet accessed 1995–2001; Simon Swain, *Hellenism and Empire: Language, Classicism, and Power in the Greek World, AD 50–250* (New York: Oxford University Press, 1996), 357–79.

8. Roger French, *Ancients and Moderns in the Medical Sciences: From Hippocrates to Harvey* (Burlington, Vt.: Ashgate, 2000), 109. Building on earlier Hippocratic conceptions, Galen believed that human health required equilibrium between the four main bodily fluids, or humours—blood, yellow bile, black bile, and phlegm. The humours consisted of the four elements and displayed two of the four primary qualities: hot, cold, wet, and dry. Unlike his predecessor, Hippocrates, Galen argued that humoral imbalances were located in specific organs, as well as in the body as a whole. This modification of the theory helped physicians make more precise diagnoses and aided their prescription of specific remedies to restore the body's balance.

9. Donald K. Freedheim, ed., *Handbook of Psychology, Vol. 1 History of Psychology* (Hoboken, N.J.: Wiley, 2003), 307.

10. Lois N. Magner, *A History of the Life Sciences: Third Edition, Revised and Expanded* (New York: Marcel Dekker, 2002), 244.

11. Fritjof Capra, *The Turning Point* (New York: Simon & Schuster, 1982), 107–8.

12. Isaac Newton, *The Principia: Mathematical Principles of Natural Philosophy* (Berkeley: University of California Press, 1999), 379–83.

13. *Isaac Newton Philosophical Writings: Cambridge Texts in the History of Philosophy Series*, ed. Andrew Janiak (Cambridge: Cambridge University Press, 2004), 117. Leibniz, Newton's contemporary, laughed at this suggestion, asserting that an omnipotent God could wind up the clock once and then could

sit back and watch it run. Leibniz's views influenced the eighteenth-century Deists who acknowledged a creator but, in a break with the notion of micromanagement, doubted whether God retained much day-to-day interest in creation.

14. William Blake, in a letter to T. Butts, dated November 22, 1802, in *The Complete Poetry and Prose of William Blake*, New and Revised Edition, ed. David V. Erdman (Berkeley: University of California Press, 1982), 720.

15. Rudolf Steiner, *Nature's Open Secrets: Introduction to Goethe's Scientific Writings* (Great Barrington, Mass.: Steiner Books, 2000), 56–63.

16. Robert Richards, *The Romantic Conception of Life: Science and Philosophy in the Age of Goethe* (Chicago: University of Chicago Press, 2002), 453–57; hereafter cited as *Romantic Conception*.

17. Theodore Rozsak, *Where and When the Wasteland Ends* (New York: Doubleday, 1972), 329. See also Donna Haraway, *Crystals, Fabrics, and Fields: Metaphors of Organicism in Twentieth-Century Developmental Biology* (New Haven: Yale University Press, 1976).

18. Richards, *Romantic Conception*, 430.

19. Robert Richards, "Michael Ruse's Design for Living," in *Journal of the History of Biology* 37 (2004): 27.

20. Immanuel Kant, *Critique of Judgment*, trans. J. H. Bernard, introd. Marc Lucht (New York: Barnes and Noble, 2005), 178.

21. Johannes Wolfgang von Goethe, "One and All," in *Collected Works: Selected Poems*, Vol. 1, ed. Christopher Middleton, trans. Michael Hamburger (Princeton: Princeton University Press, 1994), 241; hereafter cited as *Selected Poems*.

22. Ibid., 159.

23. Johann Wolfgang von Goethe, *Scientific Studies*, ed. and trans. Douglas Miller (Princeton: Princeton University Press, 1995), 121.

24. R. H. Stephenson, *Goethe's Conception of Knowledge and Science* (Edinburgh: Edinburgh University Press, 1995), 68.

25. Goethe, "Epirrhema" in *Selected Poems*, 159.

26. Elizabeth A. Williams, *A Cultural History of Medical Vitalism in Enlightenment Montpellier* (Burlington, Vt.: Ashgate, 2003), 12.

27. Justus Liebig, *Animal Chemistry or Organic Chemistry in its Application to Physiology and Pathology*, trans. W. Gregory (Cambridge: John Owen, 1842).

28. Ibid., 199.

29. Rainer Schubert-Soldern, *Mechanism and Vitalism: Philosophical Aspects of Biology* (London: Burns & Oates, 1962); Ludwig von Bertralanfly, "Biology as the Central Science," in *From Gaia to Selfish Genes: Selected Writings in the Life Sciences*, ed. Connie Barlow (Cambridge: MIT Press, 1996), 104–7.

30. Hans Driesch, *Science and Philosophy of the Organism*, Vol. II (London: Adamand Charles Black, 1908), 197, 205.

31. Ibid., 192. See also Hans Driesch, *The History and Theory of Vitalism* (London: Macmillan, 1914), 39.

32. Henri Bergson, *Creative Evolution* (New York: Henry Holt, 1911).

33. Henri Bergson, *Time and Free Will,* trans. F. L. Pogson (London: Macmillan, 1913), 101.

34. Henri Bergson, *The Two Sources of Morality and Religion,* trans. R. A. Audra and C. Bereton with W. H. Carter (New York, Henry Holt, 1935).

35. Ibid., 49, 67ff.

36. Richard Lofthouse, *Vitalism in Modern Art, c. 1900–1950: Otto Dix, Stanley Spencer, Max Beckmann, and Jacob Epstein* (Lewiston, N.Y.: Edwin Mellen Press, 2005). This study sketches the wider history of vitalism in order to explain why it assumed such a remarkable force in the modernist period, and then refines the theme by tracing vitalism in modern art, focusing on four major vitalist artists, the German painters Otto Dix and Max Beckmann, the English painter Stanley Spencer, and the Polish-American sculptor Jacob Epstein.

37. Charles Birch and John Cobb, *The Liberation of Life: From the Cell to the Community* (Denton, Tex.: Environmental Ethics Books, 1990).

38. Capra, *The Turning Point,* 53, 107–8.

CHAPTER 5

1. Alfred N. Whitehead, *Process and Reality,* corrected edition, ed. David Ray Griffin and Donald W. Sherburne (New York: Free Press, 1978), 79.

2. Henry Bergson, *Creative Evolution* (New York: Henry Holt, 1911), 47.

3. Whitehead, *Process and Reality,* 18–20; 80–87.

4. Alfred N. Whitehead, *Adventures of Ideas* (New York: Macmillan, 1929), 53.

5. Ibid., 201.

6. Whitehead, *Process and Reality,* 22–24; 52; 234; 243–45.

7. Anne Conway, *The Principles of the Most Ancient and Modern Philosophy,* ed. Allison P. Coudert and Taylor Corse (Cambridge: Cambridge University Press, 1996), 46–48; hereafter cited as *Principles.*

8. Alfred N. Whitehead, *The Function of Reason* (Princeton: University Press, 1929), 8.

9. Henry Nelson Wieman, *Man's Ultimate Commitment* (Carbondale and Edwardsville: Southern Illinois University Press, 1958), 12.

10. Henry Nelson Wieman and Regina Wescott Wieman, *Normative Psychology of Religion* (New York: Thomas Y. Crowell, 1935), 46.

11. Ibid., 52.

12. Henry Nelson Wieman, *The Source of Human Good* (Carbondale and Edwardsville: Southern Illinois University Press, 1946), 58. It is important to note that even though Wieman confined his discussion of the creative event as it occurs chiefly in communication between human individuals, he viewed the universe as being composed of an infinitely complex structure of events, and he affirmed that creative interaction occurs in all organisms. He wrote, "The thin layer of structure characterizing events knowable to the human mind by way of linguistic specification is very thin indeed compared to that

massive, infinitely complex structure of events, rich with quality, discriminated by the non-cognitive feeling-reactions of associated organisms human and nonhuman" (66).

13. Ibid., 303.

14. Ibid., 68.

15. Conway, *Principles*, 48.

16. Wieman, *The Source of Human Good*, 8.

17. Conway, *Principles*, 39–40; 45–48.

18. Ibid., 47.

19. Wieman, *The Source of Human Good*, 182.

20. Conway, *Principles*, 47.

21. Wieman, *The Source of Human Good*, 299.

22. Henry Nelson Wieman and Walter Marshall Horton, *The Growth of Religion* (Chicago: Willett, Clark, 1938), 368.

23. Wieman, *Man's Ultimate Commitment*, 305.

24. Conway, *Principles*, 47.

25. Wieman, *The Source of Human Good,* 201.

26. Ibid., 73.

27. Ibid., 92.

28. Ibid., 301.

CHAPTER 6

1. Francis Bacon, *The New Organon*, ed. Lisa Jardine and Michael Silverthorne (Cambridge: Cambridge University Press, 2000). Restoration science was self-consciously Baconian; it adherents were passionately devoted to the inductive method articulated by Bacon in the early seventeenth century as a means of superceding the sterile scholastic science of his day. Yet Restoration science was controversial in its time in spite of its crucial advances in the classification and study of plant and animal life, in the understanding of human physiology, pneumatics, optics, and other problems.

2. Francis Bacon, *The Advancement of Learning and the New Atlantis* (London: Oxford University Press, 1906).

3. Carolyn Merchant, *The Death of Nature: Women, Ecology and the Scientific Revolution* (New York: HarperCollins, 1980), 165.

4. Elizabeth A. Williams, *A Cultural History of Medical Vitalism in Enlightenment Montpellier* (Burlington, Vt.: Ashgate, 2003), 12.

5. Pierre Roussel, *Systeme physique et moral de la femme* (Paris: Vincent, 1775), 6–7. Some other discussions related to the equality of the sexes were based on a Galenic model of physiological homology between male and female reproductive organs, in which the lesser vital heat of women made them lesser versions of men.

6. Katharina Rowold, ed., *Gender and Science: Late Nineteenth-Century Debates on the Female Mind and Body* (Bristol, England: Thoemmes Press, 1996), xvii.

7. Ibid., 180–81.

8. Charles Darwin, *The Descent of Man, and Selection in Relation to Sex* (New York: Prometheus Books, 1998 [1871/1874]).

9. Ibid., 583.

10. Ibid., 583–84. See also Evelleen Richards, "Darwin and the Descent of Woman," in *The Wider Domain of Evolutionary Thought,* ed. David Oldroyd and Ian Langham (London: D. Reidel, 1983), 57–111.

11. John Stuart Mill, "On the Subjugation of Women," in *Feminism: The Essential Historical Writings,* ed. Miriam Schneir (New York: Vintage Books, 1994), 70–71. Mill wrote that available knowledge did not warrant the absolute certainty that most people assumed when stating the essential differences between the sexes. He also contended that since women were prohibited in using their faculties, it was impossible to know what was nature and what was nurture in the differences between women and men.

12. Georges Louis Leclerc Comte de Buffon, *Buffon's Natural History of Man, the Globe, and of Quadrupeds* (New York: Leavitt & Allen: 1853). See also *From Natural History to the History of Nature: Readings from Buffon and his Critics,* ed., trans., and introd. John Lyon and Philip R. Sloan (South Bend: University of Notre Dame Press, 1981).

13. Arthur Gobineau, *The Inequality of Human Races* (1853), preface by George L. Mosse (New York: H. Fertig, 1999); Houston Stewart Chamberlain, *Race and Civilization,* trans. A. S. Levetus and W. Entz (London: K. Paul Trench, Trubner and Co., ltd.; New York: Macmillan, 1928); Geoffrey Field, *Evangelist of Race: The Germanic Vision of Houston Stewart Chamberlain* (New York: Columbia University Press, 1981).

14. John P. Jackson, Jr. and Nadine Weidman, eds., *Race, Racism, and Science* (Santa Barbara: ABC-CLIO, 2004), 34. For further reading, see Peter Reill, "Anti-Mechanism, Vitalism, and their Political Implications in Late Enlightened Scientific Thought," *Francia* 16 (1989): 195–212; Elazar Parkan, *The Retreat of Scientific Racism: Changing Concepts of Race in Britain and the United States Between the World Wars* (Cambridge: Cambridge University Press, 1992); George Fredrickson, *The Black Image in the White Mind: The Debate on Afro-America Character and Destiny, 1817–1914* (Hanover: Wesleyan University Press, 1987); Stephen J. Gould, *The Mismeasure of Man* (New York: W.W. Norton, 1981); Nancy Stepan, *The Idea of Race in Science: Great Britain, 1800–1960* (London: Macmillan, 1982).

15. Michel Foucault, *Power/Knowledge: Selected Interviews and Other Writings, 1972–77* (New York: Pantheon, 1980), 81–82.

16. Carol Wayne White, *Poststructuralism, Feminism, and Religion: Triangulating Positions* (Amherst, N.Y: Humanity Books, 2002), 8–9.

17. Recent studies in critical race theory show that even though such terms as blackness and whiteness are constructions that are projected, they take on certain meanings that apply to certain groups of people in such a way that makes it difficult not to think of those people without certain affectively charged associations. Thus, the blackness and whiteness of individuals and

groups become regarded by a racist culture, which take their associations too seriously, as their essential features—as, in fact, material features of their being. For further reading, see Robert J. C. Young, *Colonial Desire: Hybridity in Theory, Culture, and Race* (London and New York: Routledge, 1995); Emmanuel Eze, *Race and the Enlightenment: A Reader* (Malden, Mass.: Blackwell, 2000); Kwame Anthony Appiah, "Racisms," in *Anatomy of Racism*, ed. David Theo Goldberg (Minneapolis: University of Minnesota Press, 1990), 3–17; Paul Gilroy, *The Black Atlantic: Modernity and Double Consciousness* (Cambridge: Harvard University Press, 2007).

18. Frantz Fanon, *Wretched of the Earth* (New York: Grove Press, 1968), 311–12. See also Frantz Fanon, *Black Skin, White Masks*, trans. Charles Lamm Markmann (New York: Grove Press, 1967); Amie Cesaire, *Discourse on Colonialism*, trans. John Pinkham (New York: Monthly Review Press, 1972), 10.

19. Catherine Keller and Ann Daniell, eds., *Process and Difference* (Albany: State University of New York Press, 2002); Douglas Sturm, ed., *Belonging Together: Politics and Faith in a Relational World* (Claremont, Calif.: P & F Press, 2003); John Cobb and John Birch, *The Liberation of Life: From the Cell to the Community* (Denton, Tex.: Environmental Ethics Books, 1990).

20. Christina Crosby, "Dealing with Differences," in *Feminists Theorize the Political*, ed. Judith Butler and Joan W. Scott (New York: Routledge, 1992), 130–43; Elizabeth Spelman, "Simone Beauvoir and Women: Just Who Does She Think 'We' Is?" in *Feminist Interpretations and Political Theory*, ed. Carol L. Shanley and Carole Pateman (University Park: Pennsylvania State University Press, 1991), 199–214; Rosi Braidotti, *Patterns of Dissonance* (New York: Routledge, 1991), 86–97; 209–73; Genevieve Lloyd, *The Man of Reason: "Male" and "Female" in Western Philosophy* (Minneapolis: University of Minnesota Press, 1984), 104–9; Rosi Braidotti, "Ethics Revisited: Women and/in Philosophy," in *Feminist Challenges: Social and Political Theory*, ed. Carole Pateman and Elizabeth Gross (Boston: Northeastern University Press, 1986), 44–60; Elizabeth D. Harvey and Kathleen Okruhlik, eds., *Women and Reason* (Ann Arbor: University of Michigan Press, 1992).

21. Sandra Harding, *The Science Question in Feminism* (Ithaca: Cornell University Press, 1986), 238. See also Jane Duran, *Toward a Feminist Epistemology* (Savage, Md.: Rowman & Littlefield Publishers, Inc, 1991); Sandra Harding, *Whose Science? Whose Knowledge?* (Ithaca: Cornell University Press, 1991); Nancy Tuana, ed., *Feminism & Science* (Bloomington: Indiana University Press, 1989); Lynn Hankinson Nelson, *Who Knows: From Quine to a Feminist Empiricism* (Philadelphia: Temple University Press, 1990); Helen Longino, *The Fate of Knowledge* (Princeton: Princeton University Press, 2001) and *Science as Social Knowledge* (Princeton: Princeton University Press, 1990); Elizabeth Potter, *Gender and Boyle's Law of Gases* (Bloomington: Indiana University Press, 2001).

22. For another important figure whose writings helped to inaugurate critical feminist appraisals of problematic Christian conceptualizations, see Mary Daly, *Beyond God the Father: Toward a Philosophy of Women's Liberation* (1973: reissued with an "Original Reintroduction by the Author," Boston: Beacon

Press, 1985); *Pure Lust: Elemental Feminist Philosophy* (Boston: Beacon Press 1984; San Francisco HarperSanFrancisco, 1992). Additionally, Catherine Keller's synthesizing work in postmodernism, constructive theology, and ecological studies has yielded some of the most provocative and creative critical perspectives in contemporary feminist religious thought. For further reading, see Catherine Keller, *Face of the Deep: A Theology of Becoming* (New York: Routledge, 2003); *From a Broken Web* (Boston: Beacon Press, 1988); Catherine Keller and Laurel Kearnes, eds., *Ecospirit: Religions and Philosophies for the Earth* (New York: Fordham University Press, 2007).

23. Rosemary R. Ruether, *New Women/New Earth: Sexist Ideologies and Human Liberation* (Boston: Beacon Press, 1995 [1971]), 204.

24. Ibid, 188–96.

25. Rosmary R. Ruether, *To Change the World* (Eugene, Ore.: Wipf & Stock, 2001), 60.

26. See Rosemary R. Ruether, *Gaia and God: An Ecofeminist Theology of Earth Healing* (San Francisco: Harper and Row, 1992); Rosemary R. Ruether, *Women Healing Earth: Third World Women on Ecology, Feminism, and Religion* (Maryknoll, N.Y.: Orbis Books, 1996); Rosemary R. Ruether and Dieter T. Hessel, eds., *Christianity and Ecology: Seeking the Well Being of Earth and Humans* (Cambridge: Harvard University Press: 2000); Rosemary R. Ruether, *Integrating Ecofeminism Globalization and World Religions* (Savage, Md.: Rowman and Littlefield, 2005); Christine J. Cuomo, *Feminism and Ecological Communities: An Ethic of Flourishing* (London: Routledge, 1998); Greta Gaard, ed., *Ecofeminism: Women, Animals, and Nature* (Philadelphia: Temple University Press, 1993); Noel Sturgeon, *Ecofeminist Natures: Race, Gender, Feminist Theory, and Political Action* (London: Routledge, 1997); Karen J. Warren, ed., *Ecological Feminist Philosophies* (Bloomington: Indiana University Press, 1996).

27. Rosemary R. Ruether, *Gaia and God: An Ecofeminist Theology of Earth Healing* (San Francisco: HarperCollins: 1992), 250; hereafter cited as *Gaia and God*.

28. Ibid.

29. Mark C. Taylor, *Erring/A/Theology* (Chicago: University of Chicago Press, 1986), 30.

30. Ruether, *Gaia and God*, 253.

31. Charles Darwin, *On the Origin of the Species*, ed. and introd. David Knight (London/New York: Routledge 2003 [1859]), 61.

32. Ibid., 63. See also Charles Darwin, "Notebook D," in *On Evolution*, ed. Thomas Glick and David Kohn (Indianapolis: Hackett, 1996), 73–74.

33. Sue Rosser, *Biology and Feminism* (New York: Twayne, 1992), 56. See also Ruth Bleir, "Biology and Women's Policy: A View from the Biological Sciences," in *Women, Biology and Public Policy*, ed. Virginia Sapiro (Beverly Hills, Calif.: Sage, 1985), 21; Hilary Rose and Steve Rose, eds., *Alas, Poor Darwin: Arguments against Evolutionary Psychology* (London: Jonathan Cape, 2000), 109.

34. Thomas Malthus, *An Essay on the Principle of Population* (New York/London: W.W. Norton, 1976 [1798]).

35. Edmund Spencer, *Social Statics; or, The Conditions Essential to Human Happiness Specified, and the First of Them Developed* (London: J. Chapman, 1851), 323.

36. Donna Haraway, *Simians, Cyborgs, and Women* (London: Free Association Press, 1991); Ruth Hubbard, *The Politics of Women's Biology* (New Brunswick: Rutgers University Press, 1990); Lynne Segal, *Why Feminism?* (New York: Columbia University Press, 1990).

37. Irene Diamond and Lee Quinby, eds., *Feminism & Foucault: Reflections on Resistance* (Boston: Northeastern University Press, 1988), xi.

38. Mary Midgley, *Evolution as a Religion* (London/New York: Methuen, 1985), 3–4.

39. Sandra Harding, *Is Science Multicultural? Postocolonialism, Feminism, and Epistemologies* (Bloomington: Indiana University Press, 1998), 39, 56.

40. James B. Ashbrooke and Carol Albright, *The Humanizing Brain: Where Religion and Neuroscience Meet* (Cleveland: Pilgrim Press, 1997), 71ff.

41. For assorted contemporary debates, see Jane Maienschein and Michael Ruse, eds., *Biology and the Foundation of Ethics* (Cambridge: Cambridge University Press, 1999); Paul Lawrence Farber, *The Temptations of Evolutionary Ethics* (Berkeley: University of California Press, 1998); Robert Wright, *The Moral Animal: Why We Are, The Way We Are: The New Science of Evolutionary Psychology* (New York: Vintage, 1995); Richard Dawkins, *The Selfish Gene* (Oxford: Oxford University Press, 1989); Edward O. Wilson, *On Human Nature* (Cambridge: Harvard University Press, 1988); Edward O. Wilson, *Sociobiology: The New Synthesis* (Cambridge: Belknap Press of Harvard University Press, 2000); Gabriel Dover, *Dear Mr. Darwin: Letters on the Evolution of Life and Human Nature Berkeley* (Berkeley: University Press, 2000).

42. Ursula Goodenough, *The Sacred Depths of Nature* (Oxford/New York: Oxford University Press, 1998), 63.

43. Ibid., 64.

44. Ian Barbour, *Nature, Human Nature, God* (Minneapolis: Fortress Press, 2002), 71.

45. Michael Arbib, *The Metaphorical Brain 2: Neural Networks and Beyond* (New York: Wiley, 1989); Joseph LeDoux, *The Emotional Brain: The Mysterious Underpinnings of Emotional Life* (New York: Simon & Schuster, 1996); Leslie A. Brothers, *Friday's Footprint: How Society Shapes the Human Mind* (New York: Oxford University Press, 1997).

46. Konstantin Kolenda, *Religion Without God* (Buffalo: Prometheus Books, 1976), 76.

47. Emily Dickinson, "Poem 657," *Complete Poems of Emily Dickinson*, ed. Thomas H. Johnson (Boston: Little, Brown, 1957).

48. Alfred North Whitehead, *Science and the Modern World* (New York: Macmillan, 1926), 34.

49. Mark C. Taylor, *Erring; A Postmodern A/theology* (Chicago: University of Chicago Press, 1984), 130.

50. Ibid., 138.

51. Goodenough, *The Sacred Depths of Nature*, 73.

Bibliography

Arbib, Michael. *The Metaphorical Brain 2: Neural Networks and Beyond*. New York: John Wiley, 1989.

Aristotle. *The Metaphysics: Aristotle*. Great Books in Philosophy. Translated by John H. McMahon. Amherst, N.Y.: Prometheus Books, 1991.

Ashbrooke, James B., and Carol Albright. *The Humanizing Brain: Where Religion and Neuroscience Meet*. Cleveland: Pilgrim Press, 1997.

Bacon, Francis. *Novum Organum*. Vol. IV. In *The Works of Francis Bacon*. 14 Vol. Edited by J. Spedding, R. L. Ellis, and D. D. Heath. London: 1857–1874.

———. *The Advancement of Learning and the New Atlantis*. London: Oxford University Press, 1906.

———. *New Organon*. Edited by Lisa Jardine and Michael Silverthorne. Cambridge: Cambridge University Press, 2000.

Bailey, Richard. *New Light on George Fox and Early Quakerism*. San Francisco: Mellen Research University Press, 1992.

Barbour, Hugh. *The Quakers in Puritan England*. With a foreword by Roland Bainton. New Haven: Yale University Press, 1964.

Barbour, Hugh, and Arthur Roberts, eds. *Early Quaker Writings, 1650–1700*. Grand Rapids, Mich.: William B. Eerdmans, 1973.

Barbour, Ian. *Nature, Human Nature, God*. Minneapolis: Fortress Press, 2002.

Barlow, Connie, ed. *From Gaia to Selfish Genes: Selected Writings in the Life Sciences* Cambridge: MIT Press, 1996.

Barrett, Michelle, and Anne Phillips. *Destabilizing Theory*. Palo Alto: Stanford University Press, 1992.

Bergson, Henri. *Creative Evolution*. New York: Henry Holt, 1911.

———. *Time and Free Will*. Translated by F. L. Pogson. London: Macmillan, 1913.

———. *The Two Sources of Morality and Religion*. Translated by R. A. Audra and C. Bereton with W. H. Carter. New York, Henry Holt, 1935.

Birch, Charles, and John Cobb. *The Liberation of Life: From the Cell to the Community*. Denton, Tex.: Environmental Ethics Books, 1990.

Blake, William. *The Complete Poetry and Prose of William Blake*. New and Revised Edition. Edited by David V. Erdman. Berkeley: University of California Press, 1982.

Braidotti, Rosi. "Ethics Revisited: Women and/in Philosophy." In *Feminist Challenges: Social and Political Theory*, ed. Carole Pateman and Elizabeth Gross, 44–60. Boston: Northeastern University Press, 1986.

———. *Patterns of Dissonance*. New York: Routledge, 1991.

Brooke, John Hedley. *Science and Religion: Some Historical Perspectives*. Cambridge: Cambridge University Press, 1991.

Brothers, Leslie A. *Friday's Footprint: How Society Shapes the Human Mind*. New York: Oxford University Press, 1997.

Brown, Stuart. "Leibniz and More's Cabbalistic Circle." In *Henry More (1614–1687): Tercentenary Studies*, ed. Sarah Hutton, 77–95. Dordrecht: Kluwer, 1990.

Buffon, Georges Louis Leclerc Comte de. *Buffon's Natural History of Man, the Globe, and of Quadrupeds*. New York: Leavitt & Allen, 1853.

Capra, Fritjof. *The Turning Point*. New York: Simon & Schuster, 1982.

Cesaire, Amie. *Discourse on Colonialism*. Translated by John Pinkham. New York: Monthly Review Press, 1972.

Chamberlain, Houston Stewart. *Race and Civilization*. Translated by A. S. Levetus and W. Entz. London: K. Paul Trench, Trubner and Co., ltd.; New York: Macmillan, 1928.

Cohen, S. Marc, Patricia Curd, and C. D. C. Reeve, eds. *Readings in Ancient Greek Philosophy: From Thales to Aristotle*. Indianapolis/Cambridge: Hackett, 2005.

Conway, Anne. *The Principles of the Most Ancient and Modern Philosophy*. Translated and edited by Allison P. Coudert and Taylor Corse. Cambridge: Cambridge University Press, 1996.

Coudert, Allison. "A Quaker-Kabbalist Controversy: George Fox's Reaction to Francis Mercury van Helmont." *Journal of the Warburg and Courtauld Institutes* XXXIX (1976): 171–89.

———. *Leibniz and the Kabbalah*. Dordrecht: Kluwer, 1995.

———. *The Impact of the Kabbalah in the Seventeenth Century: The Life and Thought of Francis van Helmont (1614–1698)*. Leiden: E. J. Brill, 1998.

Crawford, Patricia. *Women and Religion in England 1500–1720*. New York: Routledge, 1993.

Crosby, Christina. "Dealing with Differences." In *Feminists Theorize the Political*, ed. Judith Butler and Joan W. Scott, 130–43. New York: Routledge, 1992.

Cuomo, Christine J. *Feminism and Ecological Communities: An Ethic of Flourishing*. London: Routledge, 1998.

Daly, Mary. *Beyond God the Father: Toward a Philosophy of Women's Liberation*. Boston: Beacon Press, 1973. Reissued with an "Original Reintroduction by the Author," 1985.

———. *Pure Lust: Elemental Feminist Philosophy*. Boston: Beacon Press 1984. Reprint San Francisco: HarperSanFrancisco, 1992.

Dan Joseph, ed. *The Christian Kabbalah: Jewish Mystical Books and their Christian Interpreters*. Cambridge: Harvard College Library, 1997.

Darwin, Charles. *The Descent of Man, and Selection in Relation to Sex*. New York: Prometheus Books, 1998 [1871/1874].

———. *On the Origin of the Species*. Edited and introduced by David Knight. London/New York: Routledge, 2003 [1859].

Dawkins, Richard. *The Selfish Gene*. Oxford; New York: Oxford University Press, 1989.

Descartes, Rene. *Discourse on the Method of Rightly Conducting One's Reason and Seeking the Truth in the Sciences*. In *The Philosophical Works of Descartes*. Translated by John Cottingham, Robert Stoothoff, and Dugald Murdoch. Cambridge: Cambridge University Press, 1985.

———. *Philosophical Letters*. Translated by Anthony Kenny. Minneapolis: University of Minnesota Press, 1970.

Diamond, Irene, and Lee Quinby, eds. *Feminism & Foucault: Reflections on Resistance*. Boston: Northeastern University Press, 1988.

Dickinson, Emily. *Complete Poems of Emily Dickinson*. Edited by Thomas H. Johnson. Boston: Little, Brown, 1957.

Driesch, Hans. *Science and Philosophy of the Organism*. Vol. II. London: Adamand Charles Black, 1908.

———. *The History and Theory of Vitalism*. London: Macmillan, 1914.

Drob, Sanford. *Kabbalist Metaphors: Jewish Mystical Themes in Ancient and Modern Thought*. Northvale, N.J.: Jason Aronson, 2000.

Duran, Jane. *Toward a Feminist Epistemology*. Savage, Md.: Rowman & Littlefield Publishers, 1991.

Eze, Emmanuel. *Race and the Enlightenment: A Reader*. Malden, Mass.: Blackwell, 2000.

Fanon, Frantz. *Black Skin, White Masks*. Translated by Charles Lamm Markmann. New York: Grove Press, 1967.

———. *Wretched of the Earth*. New York: Grove Press, 1968.

Farber, Paul Lawrence. *The Temptations of Evolutionary Ethics*. Berkeley: University of California Press, 1998.

Ferguson, John. *Politics Quaker Style*. San Bernardino, Calif.: Borgo Press, 1995.

Field, Geoffrey. *Evangelist of Race: The Germanic Vision of Houston Stewart Chamberlain*. New York: Columbia University Press, 1981.

Fine, Lawrence. *Physician of the Soul, Healer of the Cosmos: Isaac Luria and His Kabbalistic Fellowship*. Palo Alto: Stanford University Press, 2003.

Foucault, Michel. *Power/Knowledge: Selected Interviews and Other Writings, 1972–7*. New York: Pantheon, 1980.

Fouke, Daniel. *The Enthusiastical Concerns of Dr. Henry More: Religious Meaning and the Psychology of Delusion*. Leiden: E. J. Brill, 1997.

Fox, George. *The Journal of George Fox*. Edited by N. Penney. Cambridge: Cambridge University Press, 1925.

Fredrickson, George. *The Black Image in the White Mind: The Debate on Afro-America Character and Destiny, 1817–1914*. Hanover: Wesleyan University Press, 1987.

Freedheim, Donald K., ed. *Handbook of Psychology, Vol. 1 History of Psychology*. Hoboken, N.J.: Wiley, 2003.

French, Roger. *Ancients and Moderns in the Medical Sciences: From Hippocrates to Harvey*. Burlington, Vt.: Ashgate, 2000.

Gaard, Greta, ed. *Ecofeminism: Women, Animals, and Nature*. Philadelphia: Temple University Press, 1993.

Galen. *On the Natural Faculties* [Computer File]. Translated by Arthur John Brock. Seattle, Wash.: Electronic Scholarly Publishing Project, 2001. Available from http://www.esp.org/books/galen/natural-faculties/html. Internet accessed 1995–2001.

Gaukroger, Stephen, John Schuster, and John Sutton, eds. *Descartes' System of Natural Philosophy*. New York: Routledge, 2000.

Gillispie, Charles Coulston. *Genesis and Geology: A Study in the Relations of Scientific Thought, Natural Theology, and Social Opinion in Great Britain, 1760–1850*. Cambridge: Harvard University Press, 1951.

Gilroy, Paul. *The Black Atlantic: Modernity and Double Consciousness*. Cambridge: Harvard University Press, 2007.

Glanville, Joseph. *Scepsis Scientifica, or the Vanity of Dogmatizing*. Edited by John Owen. London: 1885.

Glick, Thomas, and David Kohn, eds. *On Evolution*. Indianapolis: Hackett, 1996.

Gobineau, Arthur. *The Inequality of Human Races* (1853). With a preface by George L. Mosse. New York: H. Fertig, 1999.

Goethe, Johannes Wolfgang von. *Collected Works: Selected Poems*. Vol. 1. Edited by Christopher Middleton. Translated by Michael Hamburger. Princeton: Princeton University Press, 1994.

————. *Scientific Studies*. Edited and translated by Douglas Miller. Princeton: Princeton University Press, 1995.

Goodenough, Ursula. *The Sacred Depths of Nature*. Oxford/New York: Oxford University Press, 1998.

Goreau, Angeline. *The Whole Duty of a Woman: Female Writing in Seventeenth-Century England*. New York: Dial Press, 1985.

Gould, Stephen J. *The Mismeasure of Man*. New York: W.W. Norton, 1981.

Hamilton, Alistair. *The Family of Love*. Cambridge: Cambridge University Press, 1981.

Haraway, Donna. *Crystals, Fabrics, and Fields: Metaphors of Organicism in Twentieth-Century Developmental Biology*. New Haven: Yale University Press, 1976.

Harding, Sandra. *The Science Question in Feminism*. Ithaca: Cornell University Press, 1986.

————. *Whose Science? Whose Knowledge?* Ithaca: Cornell University Press, 1991.

————. *Is Science Multicultural? Postcolonialism, Feminism, and Epistemologies*. Bloomington: Indiana University Press, 1998.

Harvey, Elizabeth D., and Kathleen Okruhlik, eds., *Women and Reason*. Ann Arbor: The University of Michigan Press, 1992.

Hill, Christopher. *The World Turned Upside Down: Radical Ideas During the English Revolution*. New York: Viking Press, 1972.

————. *A Nation of Change and Novelty: Radical Politics, Religion, and Literature in Seventeenth-Century England*. New York: Routledge, 1990.

Hobbes, Thomas. *Leviathan*. Edited and introduced by Crawford Brough Macpherson. Harmondsworth: Penguin, 1968.

Hubbard, Ruth. *The Politics of Women's Biology*. New Brunswick: Rutgers University Press, 1990.

Hunter, Michael. *Science and Society in Restoration England*. Cambridge: Cambridge University Press, 1981.

Hutton, Sarah, ed. *Henry More (1614–1687): Tercentenary Studies*. Nordrecht: Kluwer, 1990.

————. "Anne Conway, Margaret Cavendish and Seventeenth-Century Scientific Thought." In *Women, Science and Medicine 1500–1700: Mothers and Sisters of the Royal Society*, ed. Lynette Hunter and Sarah Hutton, 218–34. Thrupp, Stroud, Gloucestershire: Sutton, 1997.

Idel, Moshel. *Kabbalah: New Perspectives*. New Haven: Yale University Press, 1988.

———. *Hasidism: Between Ecstasy and Magic*. Albany: State University of New York Press, 1995.

Jackson, John P., and Nadine Weidman, eds. *Race, Racism, and Science*. Santa Barbara: ABC-CLIO, 2004.

Janiak, Andrew, ed. *Isaac Newton Philosophical Writings: Cambridge Texts in the History of Philosophy Series*. Cambridge: Cambridge University Press, 2004.

Jones, Rufus M. *Studies in Mystical Religion*. London: Macmillan, 1909.

Jordan, W. K. *The Development of Religious Tolerance in England*. Vols. I–III. Cambridge: Harvard University Press, 1932–38.

Kant, Immanuel. *Critique of Judgment*. Translated by J. H. Bernard. With an introduction by Marc Lucht. New York: Barnes and Noble, 2005.

Kargon, John H. *Atomism in England from Hariot to Newton*. Oxford: Clarendon Press, 1966.

Keith, George. *Immediate Revelation*. London: 1675.

Keller, Catherine. *From a Broken Web*. Boston: Beacon Press, 1988.

———. *Face of the Deep: A Theology of Becoming*. New York: Routledge, 2003.

Keller, Catherine, and Ann Daniell, eds. *Process and Difference*. Albany: State University of New York Press, 2002.

Keller, Catherine, and Laurel Kearnes, eds. *Ecospirit: Religions and Philosophies for the Earth*. New York: Fordham University Press, 2007.

Kolenda, Konstantin. *Religion Without God*. Buffalo: Prometheus Books, 1976.

Kroll, Richard, ed. *Philosophy, Science, and Religion in England 1640–1700*. Cambridge: Cambridge University Press, 1992.

Kwame Anthony Appiah, "Racisms." In *Anatomy of Racism*, ed. David Theo Goldberg, 3–17. Minneapolis: University of Minnesota Press, 1990.

LeDoux, Joseph. *The Emotional Brain: The Mysterious Underpinnings of Emotional Life*. New York: Simon & Schuster, 1996.

Liebig, Justus. *Animal Chemistry or Organic Chemistry in its Application to Physiology and Pathology*. Translated by W. Gregory. Cambridge: John Owen, 1842.

Lindberg, David C., and Ronald L. Numbers. "Beyond War and Peace: A Reappraisal of the Encounter between Christianity and Science." *Church History* 55, no. 3 (September 1986): 338–54.

———. *God and Nature: Historical Essays on the Encounter Between Christianity and Science*. Berkeley: University of California Press, 1986.

Lloyd, Genevieve. *The Man of Reason: "Male" and "Female" in Western Philoso-phy*. Minneapolis: University of Minnesota Press, 1984.

Lofthouse, Richard. *Vitalism in Modern Art, C. 1900–1950: Otto Dix, Stanley Spencer, Max Beckmann, and Jacob Epstein*. Lewiston, N.Y.: Edwin Mellen Press, 2005.

Longino, Helen. *Science as Social Knowledge*. Princeton: Princeton University Press, 1990.

———. *The Fate of Knowledge*. Princeton: Princeton University Press, 2001.

Lyon, John, and Philip R. Sloan, eds. Translated and introduction by John Lyon and Philip Sloan. *From Natural History to the History of Nature: Readings from Buffon and his Critics*. South Bend: University of Notre Dame Press, 1981.

MacCannell, Juliet Flower, and Laura Zakarin. *Thinking Bodies*. Palo Alto: Stanford University Press, 1994.

Magner, Lois N. *A History of the Life Sciences: Third Edition, Revised and Ex-panded*. New York: Marcel Dekker, 2002.

Maienschein, Jane, and Michael Ruse, eds. *Biology and the Foundation of Ethics*. Cambridge: Cambridge University Press, 1999.

Malthus, Thomas. *An Essay on the Principle of Population*. New York/London: W.W. Norton, 1976 [1798].

Marsh, Christopher. *The Family of Love in English Society, 1550–1630*. Cam-bridge: Cambridge University Press, 1994.

McGregor, J., and Barry Reay, eds. *Radical Religion in the English Revolution*. London: Oxford University Press, 1984.

Merchant, Carolyn. "The Vitalism of Anne Conway." *Journal of the History of Philosophy* XVII (1979): 225–69.

———. *The Death of Nature*. New York: HarperCollins, 1980.

Midgley, Mary. *Evolution as a Religion*. London/New York: Methuen, 1985.

Moore, Rosemary. *The Light in their Consciences: The Early Quakers in Britain 1646–1666*. University Park: Pennsylvania State University, 2000.

More, Henry. *An Explanation of the Grand Mystery of Godliness*. London: Flesher and Morden, 1660.

———. *A Collection of Several Philosophical Writings*. Vol. I. New York and London: Garland, 1978.

Nelson, Lynn Hankinson. *Who Knows: From Quine to a Feminist Empiricism*. Philadelphia: Temple University Press, 1990.

Newton, Isaac. *The Principia: Mathematical Principles of Natural Philosophy*. Ber-keley: University of California Press, 1999.

Nicolson, Marjorie Hope, and Sarah Hutton, eds. *The Conway Letters: The Correspondence of Anne, Viscountess Conway, Henry More, and their Friends (1642–1684).* Oxford: Clarendon Press, 1992.

Nuttall, G. F. "Unity with the Creation: George Fox and the Hermetic Philosophy." *Friends Quarterly* 1 (1947): 137–43.

Owen, Gilbert R. "The Famous Case of Lady Anne Conway." *Annals of Medical History* 9 (1937): 567–71.

Parkan, Elazar. *The Retreat of Scientific Racism: Changing Concepts of Race in Britain and the United States Between the World Wars.* Cambridge: Cambridge University Press, 1992.

Potter, Elizabeth. *Gender and Boyle's Law of Gases.* Bloomington: Indiana University Press, 2001.

Power, Henry. *Experimental Philosophy, in Three Books: Containing New Experiments, Microscopal, Mercurial, Magnetical.* Edited by M. B. Hall. London: 1664. Reprint, New York: Johnson Reprint Corporation, 1966.

Reay, Barry. *The Quakers and the English Revolution.* London: Temple Smith, 1985.

Reill, Peter. "Anti-Mechanism, Vitalism, and their Political Implications in Late Enlightened Scientific Thought." *Francia* 16 (1989): 195–212.

Richards, Evelleen. "Darwin and the Descent of Woman." In *The Wider Domain of Evolutionary Thought,* ed. David Oldroyd and Ian Langham, 57–111. London: D. Reidel, 1983.

Richards, Robert. "Michael Ruse's Design for Living." *Journal of the History of Biology* 37 (2004): 25–38.

———. *The Romantic Conception of Life: Science and Philosophy in the Age of Goethe.* Chicago: University of Chicago Press, 2002.

Rose, Hilary, and Steve Rose, eds. *Alas, Poor Darwin: Arguments against Evolutionary Psychology.* London: Jonathan Cape, 2000.

Rosser, Sue. *Biology and Feminism.* New York: Twayne, 1992.

Roszak, Theodore. *Where the Wasteland Ends: Politics and Transcendence in Postindustrial Society.* New York: Doubleday, 1972.

Roussel, Pierre. *Systeme physique et moral de la femme.* Paris: Vincent, 1775.

Rowold, Katharina, ed. *Gender and Science: Late Nineteenth-Century Debates on the Female Mind and Body.* Bristol, England: Thoemmes Press, 1996.

Rudwick, Martin. "Senses of the Natural World and Senses of God: Another Look at the Historical Relation of Science and Religion." In *The Sciences and Theology in the Twentieth Century,* ed. A. R. Peacocke, 241–61. South Bend: Notre Dame University Press, 1981.

Ruether, Rosemary R. *Gaia and God: An Ecofeminist Theology of Earth Healing.* San Francisco: Harper and Row, 1992.

———. *New Women/New Earth: Sexist Ideologies and Human Liberation*. Boston: Beacon Press, 1995 [1971].

———. *Women Healing Earth: Third World Women on Ecology, Feminism, and Religion*. Maryknoll, N.Y.: Orbis Books, 1996.

———. *To Change the World*. Eugene, Ore.: Wipf & Stock, 2001.

———. *Integrating Ecofeminism Globalization and World Religions*. Savage, Md.: Rowman and Littlefield, 2005.

Ruether, Rosemary R., and Dieter T. Hessel, eds. *Christianity and Ecology: Seeking the Well Being of Earth and Humans*. Cambridge: Harvard University Press: 2000.

Sapiro, Virginia, ed. *Women, Biology and Public Policy*. Beverly Hills, Calif.: Sage, 1985.

Schefer, Peter. *The Hidden and Manifest God: Some Major Themes in Early Jewish Mysticism*. Translated by Aubrey Pomerantz. Albany: State University of New York Press, 1992.

Schmitt, Charles B. *Aristotle and the Renaissance*. Cambridge: Harvard University Press, 1983.

Schmitt, Charles B., Quentin Skinner, and Eckhard Kessler, eds. *The Cambridge History of Renaissance Philosophy*. Cambridge: Cambridge University Press, 1988.

Schneir, Miriam, ed. *Feminism: The Essential Historical Writings*. New York: Vintage Books, 1994.

Scholem, Gershom. *Major Trends in Jewish Mysticism*. New York: Schocken, 1946.

———. *Origins of the Kabbalah*. Translated by R. J. Zwiwerblowski. Princeton: Princeton University Press, 1987.

Schubert-Soldern, Rainer. *Mechanism and Vitalism: Philosophical Aspects of Biology*. London: Burns & Oates, 1962.

Segal, Lynne. *Why Feminism?* New York: Columbia University Press, 1990.

Sheets-Johnstone, Maxine, ed. *Giving the Body its Due*. Albany: State University of New York Press, 1992.

Sober, Elliot, ed. *Conceptual Issues in Evolutionary Biology*. Cambridge: MIT Press, 1994.

Spelman, Elizabeth. "Simone Beauvoir and Women: Just Who Does She Think 'We' Is?" In *Feminist Interpretations and Political Theory*, ed. Carol L. Shanley and Carole Pateman, 199–214. University Park: Pennsylvania State University Press, 1991.

Spencer, Edmund. *Social Statics; or, The Conditions Essential to Human Happiness Specified, and the First of Them Developed*. London: J. Chapman, 1851.

Spufford, Margaret. *Contrasting Communities*. Cambridge: Cambridge University Press, 1974.

Steiner, Rudolf. *Nature's Open Secrets: Introduction to Goethe's Scientific Writings*. Great Barrington, Mass.: Steiner Books, 2000.

Stepan, Nancy. *The Idea of Race in Science: Great Britain, 1800–1960*. London: Macmillan, 1982.

Stephenson, R. H. *Goethe's Conception of Knowledge and Science*. Edinburgh: Edinburgh University Press, 1995.

Sturgeon, Noel. *Ecofeminist Natures: Race, Gender, Feminist Theory, and Political Action*. London: Routledge, 1997.

Sturm, Douglas, ed. *Belonging Together: Politics and Faith in a Relational World*. Claremont, Calif.: P & F Press, 2003.

Swain, Simon. *Hellenism and Empire: Language, Classicism, and Power in the Greek World, AD 50–250*. New York: Oxford University Press, 1996.

Taylor, Mark C. *Erring; A Postmodern A/theology*. Chicago: University of Chicago Press, 1984.

Tuana, Nancy, ed. *Feminism & Science*. Bloomington: Indiana University Press, 1989.

Ward, Richard. *The Life of the Learned and Pious Dr. Henry More*. Cambridge: 1710.

Warren, Karen J., ed. *Ecological Feminist Philosophies*. Bloomington: Indiana University Press, 1996.

White, Carol W. *Triangulating Positions: Poststructuralism, Feminism and Religion*. Amherst, N.Y.: Humanity Books, 2002.

Whitehead, Alfred N. *Science and the Modern World*. New York: Macmillan, 1926.

———. *Adventures of Ideas*. New York: Macmillan, 1929.

———. *The Function of Reason*. Princeton: Princeton University Press, 1929.

———. *Process and Reality*. Corrected Edition. Edited by David Ray Griffin and Donald W. Sherburne. New York: Free Press, 1978.

Wieman, Henry Nelson. *The Source of Human Good*. Carbondale and Edwardsville: Southern Illinois University Press, 1946.

———. *Man's Ultimate Commitment*. Carbondale and Edwardsville: Southern Illinois University Press, 1958.

Wieman, Henry Nelson, and Regina Wescott Wieman. *Normative Psychology of Religion*. New York: Thomas Y. Crowell, 1935.

Wieman, Henry Nelson, and Walter Marshall Horton. *The Growth of Religion*. Chicago: Willett, Clark, 1938.

Williams, Elizabeth A. *A Cultural History of Medical Vitalism in Enlightenment Montpellier*. Burlington, Vt.: Ashgate, 2003.

Wilson, Edward O. *On Human Nature*. Cambridge: Harvard University Press, 1988.

———. *Sociobiology: The New Synthesis*. Cambridge: Belknap Press of Harvard University Press, 2000.

Windelband, Wilhelm. *History of Philosophy*. New York: Macmillan, 1910.

Witt, Charlotte. *Ways of Being: Potentiality and Actuality in Aristotle's Metaphysics*. Ithaca: Cornell University Press, 2003.

Wright, Robert. *The Moral Animal: Why We Are, The Way We Are: The New Science of Evolutionary Psychology*. New York: Vintage, 1995.

Young, Robert J. C. *Colonial Desire: Hybridity in Theory, Culture, and Race*. London and New York: Routledge, 1995.

Index

alchemy, 6, 48, 51, 64
Aristotle, 40, 57, 65, 66, 76
atomism, 41, 42, 43, 46

Bacon, 40, 68, 124n30, 128n3, 135n1;
    and empirical philosophy, 43; and
    scientific program, 98
Barbour, Ian, 114
Barclay, Robert, 19, 27, 29
Bergson, Henri, 76–79, 82, 117–118;
    and concept of élan vital, 77–78
biology, 67, 76; ancient, 66; evolu-
    tionary, 108; as organismic, 79, 80
Blake, William, 69–70
Blaykling, Anne, 38
bluestocking, 7
body: as discursive site, 31; distin-
    guished from spirit, 55–56; as
    divinized and politicized, 36; and
    dualism, 45, 58, 74, 106; and
    experience of pain, 56; in feminist
    discourse 31; as a machine, 46;
    materiality of, 34; in philosophical
    discourse, 33–35; and Quaker
    mysticism, 36–37; as sense and
    sign, 35; as trope, 32; and vital
    action, 57–58, 75. *See also* Nancy,
    Jean-Luc
Boeheme, Jacobe, 13
brain, 66, 75, 78, 107, 113

Calvin, John, 25
Cavendish, Margaret, 8, 9, 120n11
Cesaire, Amie, 102

Christianity, 29, 37, 51, 122n6;
    Calvinistic form of, 25; Church of
    England, 14; and Quakers, 16, 17,
    29, 37; as orthodox, 14, 51; as
    universal religion, 22
Conway, Anne (Anne Finch), 5, 6;
    and bodily suffering, 29, 30, 31;
    conception of love, 12, 30, 55–56,
    90, 92; conceptualization of
    nature, 55–59, 71, 81, 84, 89, 92,
    97–98; conversion to Quakers, ix,
    x, 7, 27–29; correspondence with
    Henry More, 15; critique of
    Descartes, 44, 47–48, 51–53, 56–58;
    death of, 7; doctrine of God, 49,
    50, 52, 89; doctrine of Christology,
    49, 50; doctrine of theodicy, 53;
    and early Cartesian studies, 7;
    ethical approach to nature, 4, 53,
    59, 63, 84, 90, 92, 95, 103, 118;
    illness, 4, 5, 7, 13, 14; interest in
    Kabbalah, 24, 50; monistic
    worldview, 55; mystical natural-
    ism, 51, 52, 53, 64, 71, 76, 80, 94,
    95; and salons, 11, 32; theory of
    monads, ix, 50, 52, 84; religious
    cosmology, 4, 48, 51–53, 84–85,
    89–93; rejection of Calvinism, 25;
    theory of vitalism, ix, x, 52, 57–58,
    63, 71, 85
Coudert, Allison, 26, 121n16,
    125n34, 126n41
Council of Trent, 15
Cowley, Abraham, 7

creativity, 77–78, 82, 91
Cudworth, Ralph, 6, 47, 130n28

Darwin, Charles, 75, 109–110; and
construction of gender, 100; and
notion of lower races, 100
Descartes, Rene, 3, 4, 41, 45–47, 64;
concept of body machine, 74, 98;
concept of God, 45, 46; influence
on later mechanistic theories, 67–
68, 74
Driesch, Hans, 76, 79, 116

ecohumanist naturalism, 112–118
ecojustice, 105, 107, 116. *See also*
Rosemary Ruether
Ein-Sof, 53–54. *See also* Lurianic
Kabbalah
Elizabeth of Bohemia, 27, 29, 30, 56,
121n15
Enlightenment: humanism, 64; as
ideology, 131n1; and instrumental-
ism, 102; racism of, 101; reason-
ing, 101
Evelyn, John, 47
evolutionary theory, 114; as modern
Western myth, 110, 111
experimental philosophy, 40–43. *See*
Mechanistic science

familists, 14–15, 123n81, 127n66;
compared to Quakers, 16, 18, 20;
conception of love, 14; condemned by Queen Elizabeth, 15;
perfectionism of, 14
Fanon, Franz, 102
female intellectual, 7, 28
feminist theory, 31, 32, 56, 103–105;
and critique of dualism; and
critique of science, 104, 106, 110
Fisher, Mary, 38
friends. *See* Quakers
Foucault, Michel, 32
Fox, George, 21, 26–28, 38, 127n61,
127n66; and celestial adoption,

36–37; and light within, 35; and
Quaker imprisonment, 32

Galen, 66–67, 132n8
Gassendi, Pierre, 41, 45
Glanville, Joseph, 40
gnostics, 37, 51
God: Calvinist view of, 25;
Conway's conception of, 48–49;
and creation, 22; Descartes'
conception of, 44–46; as Divine
Artisan, 40; as Divine Creativity,
85–89, 91; as *Ein-sof*, 53–54;
immutability of, 49; Quaker
silence before, 37; Quaker view
of, 35; as source of motion, 42; as
Supreme Value, 86–88
Goethe, Johann Wolfgang von, 70–
73
Goodenough, Ursula, 114, 116, 118
Greatrakes, Valentine, 6

Harding, Sandra, 112
Harvey, William, 6, 42, 130n28
Helmont, Francis Mercury van, 6–7,
9, 17–29, 48, 51; collaboration
with George Keith, 125n34;
conversion to Quakers, 27–28; as
Conway's physician, 13; intimate
friendship with Conway, 6, 7, 14;
and Keithian controversy, 126n41;
and Leibniz, 121n16; and Lurianic
Kabbalah, 124n30, 131n44; and
Quaker meetings, 18, 19, 20
Hobbes, Thomas, 3, 4, 16, 42–43,
120n11
human nature: 4, 59, 107, 112,
131n1; Conway's conception of,
53, 90, 107; modern constructions
of, 103
humanity: Conway's conception of,
25, 84; as evolution aware of itself,
117; perfecting itself, 64, 103, 105,
131n44; as prefallen, 15; as value–
laden organisms, 115–117

Hutton, Sarah, 122n1

interregnum, 14

Jones, Rufus, 15

Kabbala denudata, 23, 55, 64,126n39, 130n33
Kadmon, Adam, 50, 54
Kant, Immanuel, 70–71
Keith, George, 19, 20–27, 28; doctrine of Christ within, 20, 22; interest in the Kabbalah, 23–24
Knewstub, John, 15
Konstantin Kolenda, 115

Lavoisier, Antoine, 74
Leibniz, Gottfried Wilhelm, 9, 28,121n16, 125n30, 132–33n13
Liebig, Justus, 74–75
Luria, Isaac: concept of migration, 53; concept of transmigration, 53; concept of *Tsimtsum*, 53–54, 131n44; cosmological myth, 53–54; doctrine of "breaking of the vessels," 54; doctrine of *tikkun*, 26, 54
Lurianic Kabbalah, ix, 23–27, 50, 53–55, 90, 124–25n30. *See also* Luria Isaac

Makin, Bathsua, 8–9
Malthus, Thomas, 110
matter: as alive, 130n28; Aristotlelian conception of, 129n5; as dead, 56; as extended body, 43–45, 57; as regenerative, 26; as thinking, 34–35; vitalistic conceptions of, 56–58
mechanistic science, 4, 40–43; and primary qualities, 42; as reductionist, 57, 58; and theism, 43. *See also* Descartes
Merchant, Carolyn, 121–22n17
Mettrie, Julien de la, 67

metaphysics: of Aristotle, 66; Conway's readings in, 14, 24; and mechanistic science, 41; and process philosophy 65, 82–85; in the seventeenth century, 43; of Wieman's religious naturalism, 91–93, 94
Midgley, Mary, 111
Mill, John Stuart, 100, 136n11
Montpellier physicians, 74, 98
More, Henry, x, 5, 6–7, 12–20, 121n17; against religious enthusiasm, 15–18, 25; correspondence with Conway, 12–14, 16–20; critique of Kabbalah, 26; and Descartes' mechanism, 46–47; and Platonism, 47

Nancy, Jean-Luc, 33–36
natural philosophy, 3, 42
nature, ix–xi, 9, 12, 63–64, 128n1; 130n28; as a community, 79; ethical aesthetic visions of, 64, 69; fullness of, 71, 69; as good and valuable, 39; mechanistic view of, 41, 43; movement toward goodness, 63, 84, 85, 89; as processual, 81, 97; scientific models of, 4–5, 98; as sentient, 4, 48, 82–84
Naylour, James, 17
neoplatonism, 51, 64
Newton, Sir Isaac, 68–70, 125n30
Nicholas, Henry, 13–16
Nicolson, Marjorie Hope, 12, 27, 29, 119n1, 122n1

planetary ethics, 118
Penn, William, 19, 21, 22
Pennington, Isaac, 21
Pennington, Mary, 38
Pierce, Charles, 82
postmodern religious naturalism, x, 108; 112–118
Power, Henry, 40–41
prehension, 83–84

process philosophy, 4, 79, 81–85

Quakers, ix, x, 11–12, 14–24; compared to Familists, 16–18; as counter-cultural, 17–18, 32; as discursive text, 33; despised sect, 29; doctrine of Light within (Inner light), 22–23, 35–36; mysticism of, 23, 26, 35–38, 81, 90; persecution of, 27, 30, 32–33, 127n61; plain clothing, 18; and prelaspsarian state, 36; presence at Ragley Hall, 18–21; and Puritan influence, 35, 38, 127n62; and quaking or trembling, 36; silence before God, 37; and women preachers, 38

racism: Enlightenment, 101–102; eradication of, 118; feminist critique of, 104, 106; and scientific theories, 101
Ragley Hall, 6, 7, 9, 11–12, 18, 21–27
relationality, xi; in Conway's cosmology, 48, 64, 71, 81, 92, 95; in nature, 4–5; new forms of, 103; in postmodern religious natural- ism 105, 116–118; in Wieman's naturalism, 85, 92–93, 95
Religious Dissenters, 14
Renaissance, 40–41, 48, 128n2
Richards, Robert, 70
romantic artists, 69–70, 77
Rosenroth, Christian Knorr von, 23, 26, 126n40

Roszak, Theodore, 64
Romanes, George, 99–100
Roussel, Pierre, 99
Ruether, Rosemary R., 105–108, 117

scholasticism, 43, 49, 128n3
Shekhinah (divine spirit), 26
sefirot (vessels), 54
science: as deficient, 82, 84; as "dominion-over-nature" ideology, ix, 4; as mechanistic, 40–43; and notions of gender differences, 99; and post-Kuhnian studies, 112; and racist concepts, 101; and religion, 40, 112–113; in seven- teenth century, 3–4, 39, 40, 41; and technology, 112
Spencer, Edmund, 110–111
Spinoza, 43

Taylor, Mark C., 107
Tikkun. See Isaac Luria
transmutation, 52, 53
Tudor England, 7, 8

values, 86, 88, 91
vitalism, ix, x, 65–69, 73–80, 143n36

Whitehead, Alfred N., 82–84
Wieman, Henry Nelson, 82, 84–95, 134n12

Zeir Anpin, 23, 24
Zohar, 23

Made in the USA
Lexington, KY
28 April 2019